INTRODUCTION TO BLOCKCHAIN

ZEESHAN-UL-HASSAN USMANI

گفتگو

Gufhtugu Publications

Reach the Author: zusmani78@gmail.com

Published By:

Gufhtugu Publications, Islamabad, Pakistan

info@gufhtugu.com | **+92-340-4455990**

Join us on Social Media **@Gufhtugu**

Visit our Website: **www.gufhtugu.com**

"To make something special you just have to believe it's special."

– Mr Ping in KungFu Panda

Contents

Preface

Introduction to Blockchain has been specifically written for busy C-Level executives to introduce the world of distributed ledger technology, its disruptive impact on financial and centralized systems and massive global applications. This book is suitable for senior managers and decision makers who would like to go beyond the hype and navigate the underlying technology powering blockchain and crypto assets. This introductory book will empower business executives to identify and learn various blockchain applications, business models, opportunities and risks. It will prepare them for disruptive technologies when/where/if it is suitable for their business domains.

A lot has changed in last the 2,000 years, including the concept of money itself. It is worth mentioning that in contrast to the gradual progression of biological evolution, money has always evolved in leaps, from barter to writing on clay sheets, from commodity-based money to precious coins, from gold-backed paper currency to sovereignty-backed fiat and from digital credit-debt registers to state-issued bonds. Today, the world is standing at an opportune moment – an ever-connected environment is calling for the next jump: a form of money that is able to evolve new traits, is best suited for machine-to-machine and machine-to-human interfaces for the globalized world and enables people to conduct trust-worthy transactions without intermediaries. In a world where majority of the population has access to cell phones, while only half has access to toilets or toothbrushes, it would be quite a disappointment if money does not evolve in tandem.

Like biology, money is a historical science, where one constructs a historical narrative of a chain of events with tentative information and recorded details about the environment in which it takes place in order to explain the role, place and importance of money. The dynamics and evolution of money has always been the invisible chain of transactions and transfers among the human populace. The base DNA of world economics has changed considerably through technology in the last two decades, and the same environment that was once suitable for ~~the~~ fiat money is harming us now in more ways than we can imagine.

With respect to inventions and new technology in these last four centuries or so, Muslims have lagged rather behind. About a hundred years ago, a conference was held in Lucknow where paper currency - its use and Islamic injunctions with regard to it - was debated. Maulana Abdul Haq Haqqani had also been invited. Every few minutes, he would insist for the refreshments to be served. Naturally, this enraged the administration. Here they were, trying to arrive at some consensus regarding the wealth of the Muslim *ummah*, their *zakat* obligations and the protection of their 1400-year Islamic heritage of dirhams and dinars. And here was the Maulana with nothing but food on his mind. Just as calmly, he replied, say what you may, do what you will, paper currency will make its entrance, and once it does, it is here to stay.

Then airplane flights, use of loudspeakers, and the printing press were faced with the same indignation. For the last 200 years, the Muslim *ummah* has been unable to arrive at any consensus regarding the permissibility or non-permissibility of pictorial depictions and even of the camera.

Alas, today cryptocurrency faces the same fate. In all likelihood, nobody will really listen to my point of view. But when history evokes the various claims of *haraam*, then the tradition of Maulana Abdul Haq must also be revived. I am not even in the position to request you for food, but I may request you to just read this book instead.

And may I make another request: just hold on to this book for ten years. Time has this propensity to iron out all knots and wrinkles.

Awaiting your counsel, critique and opinion.

Zeeshan-ul-hassan Usmani
September 15, 2018

A Brief History of Money

Some thirty thousand years ago, humans lived an itinerant life, rallying sustenance from the land from wherever it could be found[1]. Drifting from place to place was the norm for man, some in search of commodities or animals, and some to escape harsh weather. After all, what needs did they have to sustain a nomadic life - a pair of clothes or two, some tools, perhaps some pottery. When they crossed paths with a neighboring tribe or clan, they would exchange one of their own goods for something of theirs - wheat in exchange for fish, a utensil or two in exchange for a blanket[2]. There existed no concept of currency, notes or legal tender - wealth was not owned in this form. Limited ownership, limited desires, communal living; life was carefree.

Competitiveness, however, is in the essence of man, and alas crept into how man began to value himself. What one owned, and how much of it, began to acquire the tinge of swagger and vanity. Wealth in the form of notes and cash was still non-existent, but the ownership of commodities and livestock was inequitably distributed. Also, people had distinct skills[3]. This disparate ownership of commodities and skills gave rise to an arrangement of mutual transactions, which we know today as the barter system. Man spent some twenty thousand years, including the Ice Ages, bartering.

In some form or another, the barter system abides in the world even today. People exchange gifts with each other, for example, or share harvests. Even today, on account of international sanctions, Iran trades various commodities from other countries in exchange for oil. In his book 'Debt: the first 5000 years[4]', David Graeber argues that the barter system is used when transactions are made between strangers, such as between people of different tribes or clans. Among the people of a certain tribe or clan, on the other hand, the sentiments of offering favors, or offering commodities on loan, prevails. Barters, and eventually currency, were used when there was a scarcity of trust; within the community, the tradition of favors or trust kept the society together[5].

Humans abandoned their nomadic wanderings in favor of permanent shelters about eleven thousand years ago[6]. Instead of viewing animals only as prey, they now began to tame and breed them. As they turned to husbandry and became cultivators of land, their personal effects and possessions began to increase. History tells us that agriculture and early human settlement began to flourish in regions of modern-day Middle East, which came to be known as the Fertile Crescent - the 'cradle of civilization'[7]. People began to divide and group themselves in terms of villages, tribes, geographical regions, races and languages. Soon, the trade of commodities between these blocs was born.

Two more thousand years passed, and from Egypt to India, from the Middle East to Macedonia, this barter system stabilized further. Anything in the world that held any value or had a demand - wheat, barley, corn, cattle, saffron, fish, and rice - was used for barter. About another thousand years passed this way. It was about ten thousand years ago that people began to count their assets. The need for this arose because the goods exchanged in the barter system were very different from each other. Consider a person with a surplus cow. He needs some saffron, but for how much saffron must he give up his cow? He now needed a way to count: a certain amount of saffron, a certain length of cloth, a certain poundage of wheat.

People began to carve likenesses of animals or commodities in clay and preserved them in clay slabs. They would draw pictures on these clay slabs[8]. Piercing a hole through these slabs, they began to wear them on their sleeve or around their necks. Much like today's soldier exhibits his conquests in the form of military badges, leaders of tribes began to display their wealth by wearing miniature likenesses of their assets on their person. Their slabs would signify the amount of animals, land or other commodities they owned. Deals were made on the basis of these.

As the barter system's popularity grew, so did its complexities. Consider this. You wish to give up your goat to acquire a few utensils, but the person whose utensils you have an eye on is in no need of a goat. What he needs are some clothes. Now you must look for a person who would trade your goat for some clothes, so that you could offer the clothes for those utensils. Then, what is the guarantee that all three of you wish to carry out these exchanges at the same time? What's more, while commodities like wheat can be measured up into any amount, what to do with a goat? If it were to be cut in half, the remaining part would immediately lose all its value.

The system evolved when with time, people unearthed new metals like gold, silver and copper. In 1100 BC, China made the first copper coins using likenesses of animals or commodities as icons. Advance a little further, and you will come across evidence that tells us how gold and silver found their use in quotidian matters. Among the various penalties in the Babylonian king Hammurabi's four-thousand year old law[9], the fine for biting a person's nose was one silver *meena* (about equal to a pound of silver). That for slapping someone was 11 *meetal* (one-sixth of a *meena*). A laborer's daily wage was a thousandth of a *meena*. In other words, if a daily-wager were to make the mistake of biting somebody on their nose, he would owe them three years' worth of wages.

Silver, particularly in Mesopotamia, and copper and gold in Egypt, began to be used as wealth. Now if a person's daily wage is a thousandth of a *meena*, then in order to measure it, he would need appropriate weights. Such weights and standards were usually kept in houses of worship. People would go there and in exchange for the wages due to them, would bring home groceries for their daily nutrition. In about the same period, Hazrat Ibrahim bought a tract in a cave (in modern-day Al-haram Ibrahimi) for the tomb of his wife Hazrat Sarah for 400 *meetals*[10], which are equivalent to about 125,000 US Dollars in today's money.

No doubt, the acquisition of gold and silver was easy for the wealthy and far more challenging for the less fortunate. For people who had neither precious metals, nor any valuable assets to barter, there was another way out. It became possible to borrow commodities and pay for them at the time of the next harvest. Clay slabs or tokens with the message '*I owe you*' began to be used for this purpose[11]. If you had borrowed ten wheat bags from somebody, you would record this on a token and give it to your lender. With the coming of the harvest, you would return what you owed to your lender and get your token back. Now if your lender needed something before your harvest came through, he was free to use your token to make an exchange with somebody else. Now you would be bound to return what you owed from your harvest to the person who was now in possession of the token. Thus began the tradition of using clay tokens to record loans[12].

There exists an inherent inequality of necessity in such transactions. The borrower is the one with the need; to the lender, it doesn't make much of a difference. From this imbalance arose the concept of interest, which Islam so forcefully thrashed some five thousand years later. You take ten bags of grain, but you must return twelve. When governments saw ordinary people making money in this way, how could they bear to be left out? As state mechanisms entered the fray, a system evolved whereby grain, for example, would be stored in temples or houses of worship, and clay tokens would be issued. Whoever took this token to the temple would be given grain in measured amounts. The state would make a profit from both the keeper and the buyer of the grain.

In 600 BC, the king of Lydia (modern-day Turkey) Alyattis introduced the world to coins. In order to make it easier for ordinary people to go about their exchanges, the current ruler would have the authority to issue a coin of a regular type, weight and value. The state kept the gold and silver - whenever the need arose, these coins could be taken to the state and exchanged for gold and silver. The equivalence of this in today's world is the promise '*the bank will pay on demand*' written on our banknotes[13].

That was the epoch when there existed many hundreds of states and rulers. Each state enforced its own standardized coins. The standardization enabled people of different countries to trade with each other - coins carried a known value, foregoing the need to weigh them each time. From the Middle East to the Chinese Black Sea, from the churches of Europe to the marketplaces of Lydia, the world adopted the currency of coins. In fact, it was in Lydia that the first marketplace where goods could be bought directly in exchange for coins was established.

When the state minted coins, it would make them slightly less than the value written on them, so that it could earn a profit. Pheidon, the 7th century king of Argos, Greece, is considered to be the first in the world to establish the weight and value of coins. The first coins that carried the seal of a ruler were minted in 700 BC on the island of Aegina. In 547 BC, the Greeks began to pay their soldiers in silver coins. This was perhaps what inspired hoards of people to join the Greek army, leading to the rapid expansion of the Greek empire[14].

Near ports of entry and exit, people - one could call them the first moneychangers - began to set up businesses where they would buy and sell coins, making immense profits for themselves. The first banker of the world was a man called Passion[15]. A slave in Greece, he gradually laid the foundations of banking, went on to acquire citizen's rights and eventually became a successful banker. When he died in 370 BC, he was in possession of 360,000 drachmas. Banking was lucrative, even then.

Coins, various types of carved objects and even knives began to be seen as a guarantee of wealth. Native Americans used their *potlatch* ceremonies as a means of exchange. The early civilizations of South America used *wampum* - beads of clam shells strung together - as currency. In 1642, the American state Virginia awarded tobacco the status of legal tender, a practice that continued for the next two hundred years[16].

Gold, silver, copper, electrum (an alloy of gold and silver) and other metals began to be used for this purpose. Between 700 BC and 400 BC, this art spread across China, Turkey, Egypt, Middle East, Europe and India. Around 412 BC, there was an idol that used to be worshipped in Rome, Italy. It even had a temple of its own and went by the name 'Monita'. Historians consider this to be the origin of the words 'money' and 'mint'. Linguists trace the root of the word 'money' from a Latin word that means 'beneficial.' When the Portuguese arrived in India through China for trade, they brought back with them Hindustani coinage, which in the South Indian Tamil language were known as '*kasu*'. This became the origin of the word 'cash'.

Soon the Romans also began to use coins. These people made use of hand carriages and the senators of the Roman Empire used slaves to carry their treasures for them. Romans started taxing their people and conquered the pieces of land one after another in quest for more money and wealth. When Macedonia falls to Romans in 167 BC, it brings back 75 million *Deenare* (300 Tons of Silver) as bounty[17].

As this immense wealth stabilized Rome and made it more powerful, the demand for luxuries arose. Romans now spent their wealth on exotic birds, slaves, horses, furniture, military goods, spices, and merchandise from China, India and Arabia. The Roman historian Pliny writes that it was in 118 BC, when Rome was ruled by money, that the first currency note of the world was born - crafted with leather, inscribed with pigments. Subsequently, 'notes of promise' were issued in various forms - on leather, tree barks, animal hides, metal plates, even bones. In the mainstream, however, the world continued to function primarily on coins, dirhams and dinars.

Owing to the high volume of imports, huge amounts of gold found its way out of Rome. For a while, while commerce was flourishing and treasuries continued swelling on account of the expansion of the empire, a time would come when this could be sustained no longer. In 117 BC, the festivities of Rome came to a halt, and money became scarcer. The state did find a solution to this - instead of minting coins of pure silver, they started adulterating them with tin or other non-precious metals. Shopkeepers were equally clever - they increased prices by the same token and thus Rome introduced the world to inflation. Poultry that was selling for 5 dinars began to cost 15 dinars, and by the following year, sold for as high as 45 dinars. The soldier who took home 225 dinars in 46 BC claimed 600 dinars in wages by 200 AD and as high as 1800 dinars by 235 AD.

In the meantime, something unique happened. On Yap, a Micronesian island in the Western Pacific, an enormous 9000-pound round stone was given the status of a deposit vault. This stone, known as the *rai* stone, was brought from the nearby island of Palau where it was quarried[18].

Picture 1: Rai Stone in the Island of Yap

The people of the Yap Island began to use the *rai* as currency - stone money. Since these stones were too large to move, the people of Yap relied on an oral history of ownership. Making a purchase with a *rai* stone simply involved consensus among the people that the ownership of the stone had changed. You could think of the *rai* stone as a large mansion. While it is not possible for the building to physical change location, its owners can certainly keep changing. You can even pawn your house to borrow money from the bank. Thus we can see that the basic foundations of our modern banking system have been extant for thousands of years.

A 'public ledger' going from person to person, made everybody aware of who owned how many *rai* stones at a particular time. Thus the people of the island, via oral tradition, kept a record of who was the owner of how much wealth. A hole resembling that of a donut was traditionally kept in the middle of this stone so that it could be carried from one place to another with the help of rods. But for all practical purposes, no physical movement of the stone was ever required.

A few hundred years passed and while transferring one of these stones from one place to another, the ship carrying it sank, and the stone fell to the bottom of the sea. This, however, made no difference. The system could continue to function as before even without the stone, and it did for the next two thousand years. The Yapese agreed that the lost stone still represented value and still belonged to the same person as before. Future transactions were settled based on the stone, even though no one ever saw it again[19].

This is very similar to how cryptocurrencies work, as the units of account in cryptocurrencies are valueless as digital objects themselves, they are only used to note value. The transactions in cryptocurrencies are also usually made by publicly announcing that from now on those particular cryptocurrency units belong to someone else. This message is sent to other users of that cryptocurrency and signed using a digital signature, which ensures that everyone can check the validity of the message, but no one can change or forge it[20].

Consider the properties of the *rai*: it was scarce, it was durable and it was not possible to make a copy of it. There is much for us to learn from this story of the *rai* stone money. This will also help us in making sense of bitcoin and blockchain.

Such a large stone is far from easy to transfer from one place to another, thus, instead of *rai*, people began to use wheat, barley and other commodities instead. In effect, the owner of the *rai* stone could trade a certain amount of wheat or barley. One currency instead of another, and thus the concept of currency trading was introduced to the world.

In the year 7 AD, in the Chinese province of Sichuan, the Tang Dynasty (618 - 907) introduced the world to the first paper currency. This was issued by some business groups together, and came to be known as '*jiaozi*'. Traders from all over the world would come to China and deposit their coins, gold or silver and would get *jiaozi* in exchange for it, which they would use to buy and sell commodities with ease. And before leaving, they would exchange any remaining *jiaozi* for coins, gold or silver[21]. You could call this a kind of people's bank which operated at the level of a province or town. Out of fear of robbery or theft, even today, small-town markets operate in a similar fashion - you go to a prominent merchant and deposit all your money with him. In exchange you receive slips of paper and you use these to make purchases from the rest of the marketplace all day long. As the popularity of *jiaozi* spread, there was the inevitable temptation among some people to fraudulently issue a surplus of this currency which was unable to be 'encashed'. Eventually, the government had to step in and take over. In 800 AD, Danish Island made the infamous law – to Pay Through the Nose[22] – where government would cut the nose of anyone refuses to pay the tax. This slang is still in use in some parts of the world for forced repayments.

In the year 1024, the Song Dynasty (960 - 1279) gave the world the first paper currency regulated by the government. Its use continued to spread and in the 12th century, this currency was issued in exchange for 26 million coins. In 1250, Florence, Italy, issued gold coinage by the name of 'florin'[23], which readily became available for local and international trading purposes.   In 1273 AD, the Yuan Dynasty (1360 - 1368) introduced a currency by the name of '*chao*'. By 1277, the use of paper currency in China was more prevalent than coinage.

In 1290, Marco Polo traveled to China and helped introduce the world to paper currency. Europe, which was still not ready to adopt currency notes, would take another three centuries to acknowledge it. It was in the 12th century AD that the first paper currency was issued in Europe. In his book, 'The Travels of Marco Polo'[24], Marco Polo writes, '*...in his entire empire, kingdom, provinces, and any realm where his power and authority extends, Kublai Khan encourages the buying and selling of merchandise using pieces of paper. Moreover, all those traders that come from India and other countries, they are not allowed to trade in coins or gold and silver. They deposit these coins in the palace of the Khan. There, Kublai Khan has hired 12 experts who establish the value of these coins, jewels, gold and silver in their own currency. They usually appraise this coinage to be far less than their true value, but there is no other recourse than to accept the deal. Additionally, this currency is immediately available, so traders take them and can buy and sell immediately. What's more, these pieces of paper are easy to carry and incredibly light.*"

Many thousands of years passed before the Chinese did to paper currency what the Romans had done to their coinage. The value of the currency kept falling; inflation kept rising. To the extent that in 1455, China had to abolish paper currency altogether. It took many hundreds of years for it to make its comeback.

In the beginning of the 16th century, when China was considering returning to promissory notes and paper currency, Europe began to reduce the size of coins in view of the rising demand. This debasement was the reason that square-shaped coins became round. According to a manual published by a moneychanger in 1606, at that time there were 341 types of silver coins and 505 types of gold coins in circulation in Amsterdam. In Europe, the first bank came into existence in 1609 in Amsterdam. The bank began to take coins in circulation, both local and foreign, from the people, and in exchange, gave people notes of guarantee equivalent to the value of these coins. This 'bank money' was a form of guarantee that the bank would pay back the owner of this note his assets, on demand. This was the first paper currency of the world which carried state backing. And legally, this was the only currency that was allowed to be used for exchange. In 1652, the Swiss government allowed a private company to open the first Swiss bank that subsequently issued the first note on 16 July 1661. The first British banknote came much later, in 1694. And America issued its own note in 1775, ten years after its independence, which came to be called the Continental Note.

Picture 2: Continental Note

Picture 3: Continental Note

In Europe, banks began the use of Bills of Exchange, which required the buyer of goods to give a note of guarantee that he would pay sometime in the future. This note required the backing of the trust of the buyer or another trustworthy guarantor. This is similar to how banks open Letters of Credit (LCs) today.

In 1640, King Charles of England confiscated the people's money kept in the Royal Mint. Traders lost their trust in the government and started putting their gold with wealth-houses in London, who had powerful safes and storehouses. In lieu of this gold, they would be given receipts and with the help of these receipts, buying and selling would be possible, since these receipts had the backing of real gold. Thus the chances of banks going bankrupt or the chances of fraud were minimized.

With time, traders gave goldsmiths the permission that if they wished, they could lend out gold, or the equivalent promissory notes to others and receive an interest on this lending. A part of this interest would also be shared with the original owners. Thus gradually, the seeds of modern banking were sown.

The Bank of Amsterdam began to give out loans to individuals and businesses, a significant proportion of these loans went to the Dutch East India Company. As people delayed in returning money or absconded, the city of

Amsterdam eventually needed to step into the management of the bank. They took over the bank in 1791 and shut it down in 1819.

The vacuum created by the sudden shutting down of the Bank of Amsterdam was filled by the Bank of England. This bank, which was established in 1694, became the world's first Central Bank, and the Pound Sterling became the world's first reserve currency. For many hundreds of years, the Bank of England remained a private bank and was nationalized only in 1946.

In Scotland in the 18th century, and in America in the 19th century, notes began to be printed rapidly. In the 19th century, over 5,000 different kinds of currency notes were in circulation in America. In comparison, approximately 800 cryptocurrencies exist in the world today.

When Christopher Columbus began his journey across the Atlantic in 1492, along with finding a path to the riches of the east, he was also looking for gold. Indeed he did find much of it - on the island of Hispaniola, near the Caribbean - but not as much as his successors found in Central and South America. In Columbus' fate was written America, after all.

When the Spanish arrived in Central and South America, they saw that the local Aztec people in Mexico and the Incas in Peru utilized gold and silver for jewelry and luxury instead of as currency. The Spanish quickly found the source of silver in Potosi, Bolivia. Here was located the largest ever silver mine in the history of the world. Between 1556 and 1783, 45,000 metric tonnes of silver were mined from here and sent to Spain. Silver mining requires the use of mercury. As a result of the insufficient availability of safety measures, many thousands of miners lost their lives. In order to make up for this shortage of manpower, slaves were brought in from Africa, a large portion of whose lives were similarly sacrificed in favor of this new-found wealth.

While this extraordinary increase in supply of gold and silver did make Spain prosperous for a while, it did not prove to be good for the future of the empire. Following the gold and silver brought into Europe by Columbus and his successors, the value of European currency declined considerably. Subsequent inflation kept a tight noose on the necks of European countries for a long time afterwards. Spain did fight some wars with this wealth, but neither did they embark upon any new trade, nor did they acquire any new skills, nor did they increase cultivation. Instead, this surplus of wealth led to inflation, severely pinching the poor. Strange indeed that the downfall of Rome happened on account of the shortage of gold and silver, that of Spain because of its abundance. In the Middle Ages, along with the decline of the Byzantine Empire, the value of their coinage declined. Gradually, the world came to adopt gold, silver or an alloy of these two metals. In the year 1717, Sir Isaac Newton (who was master of the Royal Mint at the time), created an alloy of gold and silver and completely eradicated silver from common circulation[25]

While we are on the topic of gold, let's examine it in some detail. Gold has always carried an allure for people, and has been a source of trust. Be it in the form of metal or jewelry, it has been valued by all - from the aborigines of Australia to the plunderers of Spain. The search, discovery and mining for gold took thousands of years, not to mention thousands of lives. Yet, the amount of gold that the world has so far unearthed can be fitted into a space that measures 65 x 65 x 65 feet - the size of an Olympic swimming pool. According to one estimate, the world has taken out a total of 174,000 metric tonnes of gold that is 23 grammes of gold per person on earth. We take out the entire gold from deep beneath the earth, clean it, and then have it placed in some underground vault belonging to some federal bank. Perhaps gold has some special affinity with the underground. There it lives, and their it one day takes those who use it. For thousands of years, we have been unearthing gold from the earth's crust, depositing it back under the ground in some vault, publishing promissory receipts in lieu of it, and using them like the clay tokens of China.

In the beginning of the 19th century, America began to back its currency with actual gold - the system which the world knows today as the 'gold standard.' Effectively, a country could issue only the amount of currency equivalent to the amount of gold it possessed. The country would establish equivalence against the gold, and then issue a currency. For example, if an ounce of gold in America is worth 20 dollars, it meant that each dollar is a twentieth of each ounce of gold. Anybody could go to the Central Bank, give a dollar and receive gold in equivalence to it. Following the Great Depression of 1931, the gold standard was gradually bidden adieu. Today, there is no country in the world where the gold standard still exists, whose Central Bank would give you gold in exchange for currency[26].

There are three kinds of gold standards. The first, *gold species*, in which gold coins are in common circulation and on whose basis all other prevailing currencies, are evaluated[27]. The second is the *gold bullion*, in which the basis of all prevailing currencies is gold, but gold coins themselves are not in circulation. An individual is able to buy gold in exchange of currency, but gold itself cannot be used as currency. The third, *gold exchange*, only exists between countries, and allows one country to appraise the currency of another currency based on the amount of gold in its treasury.

The currency note issued in England was being used for hundreds of years but the system of guarantee of gold behind these notes began much later. In 1821, with the guarantee of the Royal Mint, England adopted the gold species standard. United States of Canada, Newfoundland and Germany also adopted this. America introduced the Gold Eagle, and Canada the government gold. However, all countries abolished this standard at the start of the First World War[28].

America's Great Depression of 1931 became the basis of the relinquishing of the gold standard. Fearing the end of the world, people rapidly exchanged their money for gold. All the advisors of Franklin D. Roosevelt, the president of the United States, counselled him to continue using the gold standard. All but one. The President chose to listen to

George Warren, an agricultural expert, and thus America bid farewell to the gold standard. The Bank of England was near bankruptcy. Its head, Montagu Norman, upset at this situation, left for a long leave of absence. Taking advantage of his absence, his partners suddenly got rid of the gold standard one day. The rest of the world naturally had to follow the United States and England, and thus gradually the gold standard became a thing of the past. The last country to bid farewell to the gold standard was Switzerland, giving it up in the year 2000.

In 1970, President Lincoln put a restriction on the international trade of gold, thus putting a full stop once and for all on this chapter. Instead of the promise '*the bank will pay on demand*', the note '*in God we Trust*' came to be written on banknotes[29].

Right after World War II, the world did try, to some extent to adopt the gold standard once again in some form or the other, but without success. In July 1944, the Bretton Woods conference took place, in which a consensus by the name of Bretton Woods was agreed upon. One of the agreements was the establishment of the IMF, an institution that would facilitate transactions between countries. Another was that exchange rates were now pegged to gold. However, by 1960, complexities arose and by 1968, this system failed. On 15 August 1971, President Nixon took a significant measure, whereby he cancelled the direct international convertibility of the United States dollar to gold. This event, which is known as the '*Nixon shock*'[30], hammered the last nail on the coffin of the gold standard. Today, no currency in the world has the backing of gold; all currencies are *fiat currencies*, i.e. they carry the guarantee of the state.

Picture 4: Ten Dollars in Gold

Picture 5: Five Hundred Dollars in Gold

Picture 6: One Dollar in Silver

Picture 7: A Thousand Dollars in Gold

Picture 8: One Hundred Thousand Dollars in Gold

The rest was taken care of by the OPEC agreement of 1975[31]. Under the leadership of Saudi Arabia, all oil producing countries decided to use only the American dollar. Every country of the world needs oil, and now they could purchase it only in American dollars. International transactions would only take place in the American dollar therefore America could print as much of its currency as it wished without fear of devaluing it. In 1973, the price of oil was 20 dollars and rose to 100 dollars in 2012. If currency were backed by gold, the price of oil could not have risen beyond a dollar per liter.

There are many advantages and disadvantages of the gold standard. Among the advantages, the greatest is that it is based on a universal value of gold, which everybody agrees upon. Its supply is sufficiently scarce - it is neither defunct, nor too readily available like fruits and vegetables. From 600 BC to date, the status and respect awarded to gold came to the share of no other metal or element. State-issued paper currency is backed by only the trust of the people - the day that is lost, money will cease to hold any value or legal status. Such a situation is difficult to occur with gold.

The second advantage is that it limits the power afforded to the state. No state can print as many notes as it likes. The amount of notes that can be printed depends on how much gold a country possesses. When America bid farewell to the gold standard, only 48 billion dollars were in circulation in the world at the time. Today, this amount has risen to 12 trillion dollars.

Moreover, the gold standard is a democratic system which benefits producers and traders. The amount of currency in circulation will depend on the amount of gold in the vaults. Were it not for this, the government would have had much greater leeway in controlling the market in whatever way it wished. The status of the Central Bank is like an autocratic ruler. For the 'greater good of the nation', it can do anything. Not too long ago, for example, Pakistan devalued its currency against the dollar claiming that the move would help exports, but the common man had nothing to do with this decision. This is not possible in the gold standard.

Furthermore, the gold standard also safeguards against inflation. The producer and the consumer are content; only the government suffers discomfort. From the year 1893 to 1913, the inflation rate in America was stood at a mere 1.6%. After the abolishment of the gold standard, it rose from 3.3% in 1971 to 133% in 1979. According to research carried out by the American Federal Reserve, at that time, inflation in 15 countries rose from 1.75% under the gold standard to 9.17% after is abolishment[32].

Between 1971 and 2003, the American dollar lost 80% of its purchasing power. 17 cents of 1971 were equivalent to 1 dollar of 2011. By staying on the gold standard, national debt also remained low. When countries make payments in fiat currency, other countries buy national bonds in that currency. Over half of American debt is in the form of international assets. In 1971, America's total debt amounted to 406 billion dollars, which has now risen to 19 trillion dollars today[33].

Thanks to the gold standard, fewer wars were fought. According to an estimate only in the Afghanistan and Iraq wars, the United States spent 3 trillion dollars[34]. Such immense availability of money would not have been possible under the gold standard. Today, it just takes a couple of clicks for this money to be 'created'. Following the economic depression of 2008, the United States brought 3 trillion new dollars into circulation. Click... click... click... In 2008, by printing money on its own, America brought the annual supply of money from 2.6% to 152.3%[35]. From September 2007 to December 2009, whose effects were to be seen in the form of inflation in later years. But since the dollar has the support of the entire world behind it, and if the dollar drowns, it will drown many along with it. Thus the American dollar always finds the support of many people.

Under the gold standard, economic growth is also rapid. From 1792 to 1971, economic growth in America was 3.9% and fell to 2.8% after the abolishment of the gold standard. If the gold standard were in use today, American GDP would have been at least 8 trillion dollars. The gold standard also ensures against unemployment - 5% with the gold standard, as opposed to 6% without. The common man's wages are also significantly higher - 2.7% as opposed to merely 0.2%.

But there exists a group of economists who do not tire of counting the disadvantages of the gold standard. To start with, the value of gold is not stable and the rapid fluctuations that sexist in its price cannot keep the economy stable. For example, if the value of gold changes by 15% in a certain time period, the prices of goods and services will change accordingly. No society or country can agree to such instability. The price of gold decreases from 700 dollars in 1980 to 200 dollars in 1920, as the people began to make greater efforts to mine more gold. In 1933, when the world was on the gold standard, gold was valued at 563 dollars which in 1971 fell to 201 dollars. Even under fiat currency, gold prices fell from 2,337 dollars per ounce to 1,672 dollars per ounce. This trait of gold must surely be tried to be understood by critics of cryptocurrency.

The advantage of fiat currency is that one can revise the value of the currency and easily get out of an economic slump. America suffered severe economic depressions in 1884, 1890, 1907, 1893, 1931, 1930, 1932, 1933. Only in 1933, 50,000 banks shut down their businesses. But in 2008, this was dealt with much easily because the government had the power to create money.

If you affiliate a currency with any commodities, you cannot create as much of it as you want. That is why currencies today are affiliated with different baskets of commodities, and the government determines the purchasing power of a common man as what he can purchase with this amount of money.

Furthermore, inflation is deliberately incorporated into the currency, about 3%, to make sure people don't hoard banknotes. When they are aware that the value of the currency will only decrease, people have the incentive to spend rather than hoard, which has a favorable effect on the national economy.

Man can do anything for gold. Would you believe that man can go two and a half miles beneath the surface of the earth, putting one's life in danger, for a layer of gold a mere 30 inches deep? Yes, this is every day's work in South African city of Yunang. Here is located the world's deepest mine which is Witwatersend Basin. If there is gold anywhere in the world, there is a 50% chance that it came from this mine. This was discovered in 1886, and tradition is that in Vredefort Crater located nearby, whose area is 700 square miles, a crater was formed as a result of a meteor crash some 2.02 billion years ago. This mine was created or discovered under this crater.

In the Mponeng gold mine, which is located west of Johannesburg, and is owned by AngloGold Ashanti, is located the world's deepest lift. It sends 4,000 miners 2.5 miles into the ground every day. One can make sense of these numbers from the fact that 10 empire state buildings can fit in this depth. The lift operates at the rate of 40 miles an hour, yet takes 90 minutes before it reaches the first stop. Now you can only imagine what an hour and a half long journey underground in a lift is like. The temperature 60 degrees centigrade, and humidity 95%. Every day, 6,000 metric tonnes of ice is needed to quarry stones at the bottom, and this is not always available. Moreover, workers have to carry out digging underground. Ghost miners are also found here, who are trying to mine gold illegally. These people have lived underground for so long that the lack of sunlight has even changed their skin color.

Picture 9: Indian 10 Rs Note

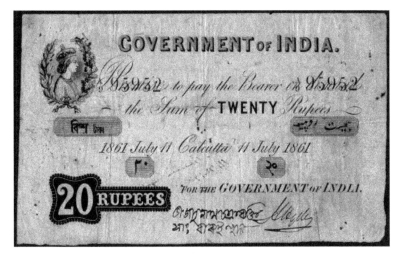
Picture: Indian 20 Rs Note

The legal miners would sell the basic necessities of life to these illegal miners for as much as 12 times the original price and this all is happening in this grave 2.5 miles under the surface.

Here, scientists have discovered bacteria called *Desulforudis Audaxviator*[36], which can make its own food and even propagate in the absence of sunlight, only with the radioactivity present in the environment.

Today, why don't these facts bother those who accuse cryptocurrency of causing environmental damage? And why stop at the mining of gold? There are many other such metals which are far more precious than gold – Rodium, Platinum. One gram of Anti-matter is worth a trillion dollars, and one gram of Anti-hydrogen costs 62 trillion dollars. In the mining of rare earth (which is used in the manufacture of iPhones), the whole resource was consumed. And its availability even today is keeping the American army in Afghanistan[37].

It is worthwhile remembering that money is a social creation. If people are backing it with their trust, it is money, otherwise it is nothing. The day that trust is gone, the paper will be worth rubbish. Moreover, each currency is limited to a society, people and community. For example, within the domain of the children's board game Monopoly, you can make purchases with monopoly money, but not outside of it. So inside the game, monopoly money is 100% legitimate money. Likewise, you cannot buy milk using the Pakistani rupee in France, while in Pakistan you may freely do so.

America's gold is preserved in various places in the shape of 1000-ounce bars. The Fort Knox bullion depository stores 4,600 tonnes of gold, whose value is estimated to be 58 million dollars. 1,781 tonnes are in West Point, New York, 1,368 tonnes in Denver and about 1,000 tonnes in the Federal Reserves. America has about 8,000 tonnes of gold of its own whose value is 100 billion dollars - also the net worth of the CEO of Amazon. Other countries of the world have also safeguarded their gold in an 80-foot deep vault of the Federal Reserves in Manhattan, New York. This is about 10,000 tonnes of gold whose value is 125 billion dollars. This is in 400 tri-ounce bars. Thus the value of a bar is 160,000 dollars. All this gold is stored in chambers, the largest of which is 10 x 10 x 18 feet and contains 107,000 bars.

Wherever in the world gold is found, whether it belonged to Africa, or was the assets of the people of Aztecs in Mexico, the wealth of the Incas in Peru, coinage of the Byzantine people, on the beds of the king of Ghana....all finds its way to this tomb under Manhattan.

The value of gold can be judged form the fact that a piece measuring 42 centimeters, which constitutes a fraction of the size of one dollar bill in size, is worth a million dollars. If Trump's total wealth of 3.7 billion dollars is converted to gold, the size of the gold slab will be 1.7 meters, shorter than the president's height. The total market of bitcoin is 14.7 billion dollars or 12.3 million ounces of gold.

Let's give a further thought to gold mining. There are those who say that cryptocurrency mining has harmful effects on the environment, that it consumes half of the world's electricity, and other such criticisms. However, consider this:

in order to mine 1 ounce of gold from the earth, 70 tonnes of waste is unearthed. Moreover, the value of all the gold in the world a mere 9.1 trillion dollars. America's debt alone is to the tune of 19 trillion dollars. The world certainly cannot afford to return to the gold standard.

There are many commonalities between gold mining and bitcoin mining. Recall California's gold rush between the years 1846 and 1852. A similar 'rush' is occurring today with respect to cryptocurrency. Gold mining was - and perhaps still is - indeed very appealing to the common man. Today, bitcoin carries the same appeal. The value of gold has more than doubled; the same is happening to the value of bitcoin. People rushed to mine gold by the hoards. From only a 100 miners in 1846, there were no less than 30,000 in 1852. Bitcoin miners have reached about 15,000 to date. Some gold miners became incredibly wealthy, others were not so lucky and still others returned home with nothing. Something very similar is happening with cryptocurrency.

Many people, who were not themselves miners, but were indirectly related to the rush, also came into wealth. Those who were selling the relevant tools, for example. Just the price of the footwear that was needed rose to as high as 36 dollars. Then there were those involved with the buying and selling of gold, gold gamblers, those who fed and housed them, and so on. The same is happening today. The ant miner mining tool that costed 2,000 dollars has now skyrocketed to 15,000 dollars. There is a three to four month wait for a graphics card. And then the technical experts and those who rent out space and electricity are also earning.

In order to make their fortunes, people also searched for gold in groups. We will all share it when it's found. This is what *pooling* is in cryptocurrency.

The greater the number of people that joined, the harder it became to find gold. Here too, the same is the case. We call it *mining difficulty*.

If you compare the energy bills of gold mining with bitcoin mining, one bitcoin expends 7 times more energy than 1 ounce of gold. But all in all, the total energy bill is still low, since the world is mining 135 times more gold than bitcoin. In 2017, at the rate of 1,800 coins a day, a total of 65,000 bitcoins were created. In comparison, the two largest companies of gold *Barrick* and *New Mont* mined 88 million ounces of gold, spending 8.5 giga joules of energy on each ounce of gold. In January 2013, the expenditure on energy, tools and expertise combined, bitcoin costed 1,800 dollars to mine. Each sell for between 14,000 and 15,000 dollars. According to a 2016 report one ounce of gold costs 1,115 dollars to take out and sells for between 1,250 and 1,300 dollars. In today's world, bitcoin mining is more lucrative than gold mining. It is, in fact, digital gold.

Let's now return to our topic. Are you aware of invisible money? It's more common than you think. Cash does not constitute even 3% of the total money of the world. The rest is in the form of digital numbers inside computers. If you have ever transferred money online, or made a payment using credit or debit cards, the numbers decreased on one side and increased on the other side. Nothing physical got transferred from one place to another. 80% of the world's currency is alive in this way. If all the people were to go to their bank to withdraw all their money, the bank will collapse. Normally, banks keep about 20% of people's deposits with them. The rest, they click click click into loans or invest in other places.

If people were to lose trust in banks, in the currency or in the government, they would immediately wish to convert it to another currency, and would rush to withdraw all their money. This is exactly what happened in Hungary in the recent past, bringing about a collapse of the economic system of the country. You may remember when in 1999, Pakistan's Prime Minister Nawaz Sharif froze all dollar accounts after the nuclear testing[38]. People's money, but they no longer had a right to it. Ever since that fateful day, the business community keeps its money out of this country. And then they are the ones taunted for having foreign accounts.

This series of money disappearing keeps appearing throughout the history, the only new thing in the realms of money is the one that you haven't read, everything else has already happened somewhere, sometime.

Consider another way in which money 'disappears'. If the inflation rate is only 3%, the price of good and services will double in 30 years. And this happens to real estate in only 10 years. People are under the impression that money maintains its value or that it is a physical asset. Both these perspectives are incorrect.

Let's look some examples that demonstrate how money lost its value.

In 1946, right after the Second World War, the Hungarian Pengo was doubling every 14 hours[39]. This meant effectively that the bread you bought on Wednesday would cost 10 times more on Monday morning. As soon as people received money, they would rush to spend it immediately, lest its value does not decrease in that time. Soon people abandoned the Pengo in favor of the barter system or the gold exchange. In August 1946, the Hungarian government introduced a new currency whose one unit was equivalent to 400 octillion 400,000,000,000,000,000,000,000,000,000 (4 x 10^{29}) Pengo. So actually, the value of the Pengo finished. People who had any savings in this currency could only use them to feel their fireplace. This is known as hyperinflation.

In November 2008, a loaf of bread in Zimbabwe costed 300 million dollars. Other countries actually had to give out notices not to use the Zimbabwe dollar in place of toilet paper. For purposes of exchange, people created their own currency and began to use it. When this currency was copied or counterfeited, people still continued using it, for who had the tools to create yet another currency? No government backing, no Central Bank, and yet the currency such that it had sufficient backing of the people's trust for it to be widely used. (Now, would you call this economy *haraam* too under Islamic Laws?)

Enter Somalia where the government is non-existent outside Mogadishu. These people also continued using *Sheligns*, whose value in the international market was no more than Monopoly money, but it remained in use, and still is.

In 1994, Brazil introduced a new currency by the name of Brazilian real.

In 2009, North Korea removed two zeros from its currency and announced that 1 won of the new currency will be equal to 100 won of the old currency. Moreover, people had only 24 hours to change their money, and one person could not change more than 690 dollars. With this announcement, people became deprived of hundreds of thousands of won. Those fateful 24 hours led to incredible sorrow for many. Officially, according to the government, 96 won equals 1 US dollar, but when you actually go to buy dollars from a moneychanger, you will get 1 dollar for 8,000 won. In exchange for your life earnings, the government handed you a mere 35 dollars. It took a single government decree to deem the rest of your money worthless. This is the government backing which we consistently ask for in cryptocurrency.

In 1923, Germany printed notes to finance its war. The dollar that could be bought for 6.7 German Marks in 1919, now its price in 1923 was 4,210,500,000,000 marks. And people began to use the German Mark in place of wallpaper.

More recently, on 3 November 2016, India worked on demonetization of its currency so that counterfeiting, terrorism and black money could be stopped. People were given a time margin of 30 days to change all 1,000 and 500 denomination banknotes. In 30 days, people managed to change 32,000 crore rupees, but many faced losses of many crores.

In Venezuela, in January 2017, one dollar could be purchased with 3,000 bolivars. By December 2017, that dollar costs 191,000 bolivars. Even though it has the largest deposits of oil in the world.

Now if these unfortunate people begin to use cryptocurrency, will you still call it *haraam*? If it still seems to you that currency notes are 'real' money compared to cryptocurrency, then let's forget about anything else and take a look at some examples from our own period.

After the 2010 earthquake in Haiti, it became difficult to distribute rations among people. Bags of rice cannot be thrown from a helicopter, for fear of injuring people. Therefore, just like many thousands years ago, the United Nations began to use houses of worship to store rations and distributed paper coupons to people. Only within 24 hours, those paper coupons began to be used as currency, as everybody knew how much ration these paper coupons were being backed by.

In many prisons even today, where banknotes are not allowed, fish, cigarettes or mobile credit are used for exchange and transactions. Children are prone to misplacing things. In schools across the United States, parents make a deposit in school canteens and children receive food coupons in exchange, which they can use just like currency in the school cafeteria. In Kenya there exists an M-PESA system by which one can make payments via mobile phone credit. In fact, 60% of Kenyans rely on M-PESA for their transactions, 30% use banks and 7% use ATMs. Now this M-PESA also has no backing of the government.

You can spend an entire week enjoying Disneyland Park on Disney tokens, can stay in a hotel using Merit Rewards, get petrol using credit card Reward Points, buy air tickets using Sky Miles even redeeming points for cash, buy clothes from Khaadi points, get loaded with Easy Paisa or send cash home, and so on. In each country and society, you will find dozens of examples where we can easily and conveniently use alternative methods in place of currency. The only important thing that is needed is the people's trust and their willingness to use it.

Yes, they work. And they work without government backing. They work without the promise of a harvest. They work without gold backing. Personal campaign, societal guarantee, or guarantee upon guarantee – these are the only sentiments needed for this system to work.

You will certainly be surprised to know that the first electronic transfer in the world took place in 1871. It was in 1851 that Western Union came into being by the name of Valley Printing Telegraph Company in New York and Mississippi. It laid telephone wires in the capital of the United States in 1861. Miscreants attacked these wires from many places and made bracelets out of them thus bringing this work to a halt. But then some of the people wearing this jewelry started getting sick. Amid fears that it was the ghosts of these 'talking wires' that had hurt them, this fiddling with the wires stopped. The first money transfer of the world happened through these telegram wires in 1871.

In 1950, a man named Frank Namara went to a restaurant to eat, but fell short of some money while paying the bill. He had to call his wife over the phone to bring cash. The embarrassment of the event, however, remained and he decided that this should never happen again. Thus Diner's Club, the first card based on credit was issued.

The first ATM machine in the world was made in 1967 by a man called John Adrian Shepherd-Barron and presented this idea to Barclay Bank. This was installed in 1967 in South London. In the early ATMs, instead of plastic cards, carbon-printed cheques needed to be inserted, and at one time, they could dispense only 10 pounds at a time.

In 1983, the Bank of Scotland gave the residents of the Nottingham Building Society the world's first internet banking service which they could use to pay their bills. And for this they needed their television and telephones. It was in 1990, with the advent of the web, true internet banking as we know it began. But the Bank of America had to wait entire 10 years for the first 2 million customers.

In 1997, Mobil Oil Corporation introduced the first contact-less speed pass card to get petrol. In 2005, credit cards introduced chip and pin numbers. Today, 50% of transactions in America and England take place on plastic money.

In 2008, Satoshi Nakomoto wrote his Bitcoin paper and in 2009, the first bitcoin transaction took place. In 2010, 2 pizzas were bought from Papa Jones in exchange for 10,000 bitcoins. And thus the world became introduced to cryptocurrency.

In 2014, Apple Pay was introduced which allows you to make secure payments without any card or wallet, and even without touching your phone. Today, in America, over 40% businesses use Apple Pay for transactions, and it seems they may be heralding the end of credit cards.

In 2015, taking inspiration from bitcoins, hundreds of cryptocurrencies entered the market using blockchain technology. Other than Canada, Japan, Australia, Estonia and Singapore, over ten countries have accepted it. In the United States, cryptocurrency is categorized as asset and is therefore taxed. In Canada, its status is that of barter. In Japan it is used as currency and legal tender, and in Australia it has the status of currency. Just like all the countries of the world sooner or later accepted paper currency, cryptocurrency too will gain acceptance around the world in one form or another.

History is witness to the fact that money has often been created to fight wars with. In 1861, the ten-dollar bill was created in America for the basic reason that the civil war expenditure could be borne. In order to deal with the civil war, President Lincoln ordered 450 million dollar notes to be printed, popularly known as *greenbacks*. In those days, all the copper of the world was being utilized for wars, so for the first time in the world, the world witnessed notes less than their value - which we know as *frictional notes*. Notes with the value 0.25, 0.15, 0.10, 0.05, 0.03, and 0.5 etc. came into the world. At one time, the American penny was made of steel, for copper was to be used for war.

We use the word 'buck' for the American dollar. Buck is actually the leather of deer, which at one point in time was used in American rural areas just like currency.

In the 19th century, many notes were counterfeit. Now, thanks to technology, only 0.01% are counterfeit. It may come as a surprise that the Secret Service came into being in 1865, only for the purpose of stopping counterfeit currency, for factories were selling banknote printing machines and dollars in the black market.

The world mines 2.5 million pounds of silver every day, amounting to 900 million pounds every year.

You can fold a normal piece of paper about 400 times. After this, it will start tearing. In contrast, you can fold a currency note 8,000 times. It is made of 75% cotton and 25% linen.

A coin's average age is 25 years, whereas the currency note is slightly different. A dollar normally lasts 5.8 years. A five-dollar note 5.5 years, ten-dollar note 4.5 years and twenty-dollar note 7.9 years, fifty-dollar note 8.5 years and hundred-dollar note's life is 15 years. According to a survey, 90% of American banknotes in circulation have traces of cocaine on them, since cash is usually in use by criminals.

Every day, 33 million notes are printed worth 54 million dollars.

Americans throw away coins worth 62 million dollars every year. And the American government issues collectible coins worth 40 million every year, which usually do not find their way in common circulation.

North Korea prints the world's largest amount of counterfeit dollars. That is the reason the design of the dollar note is constantly changed, and that is why moneychangers will charge a higher fee for old dollars than for new dollars. Nobody counterfeits a one-dollar note, as its value is low. In fact, the one-dollar note has not changed since 1929. According to American law, a banknote can only carry that personality's face who has passed away. So in case you see Obama or Trump on a banknote, be warned that the note is 100% counterfeit.

The 'continental dollar' printed in 1775 lost all its value in a mere 5 years. This gave rise to idioms that evolved as, 'not worth a continental'.

You may not have noticed, but for the last ten years or so, the world has waged a kind of war against cash. Since it is near impossible to trace or record cash transactions, this is the favorite means of transaction among criminals of the world. That is the reason many countries do not print large denomination currency notes. The weight of one million dollars is merely 10 kg or 22 pounds. Criminals transfer on average two trillion dollars from one place to another every year. Cashless transactions are recorded and also incur, in many cases, third-party fees such as bank charges.

In American, some policy experts are trying to get rid of the 50 and 100 dollar note for quite a while now. In 2014, Singapore abolished its 10,000 dollar note. Sweden gradually began to remove ATMs from rural areas so that people are discouraged from using cash. South Korea has envisioned a cashless economy by 2020. France has prohibited transactions over 1,000 pounds to be cash-based. Venezuela abolished its 100 bolivar note. From 2018, Europe has brought the 500 pound note out of circulation. Greece has prohibited any citizen from keeping more than 15,000 pounds in cash. Australia and Norway are also moving in the same direction.

Recently, when India abolished its 500-rupee note, 86% notes were retired from circulation. One person could only change up to 4,000 rupees in cash. 50% of the Indian population does not have a bank account. After this announcement, suicide and suffocation in queues took the lives of 112 individuals.

As a result of these steps, only in 2015, 426.3 million transactions of the world were cash-less. Regardless, however, even today 85% of the world's transactions are in cash.

The definition of money

The purpose behind all this exploration was to bring to light in the context of social history, the 'invention' of money, its various forms, and its value to the world. What status and necessity does money hold in each society, and were we to alter this interpretation of money, what kind of changes will evolve.

Let's try to understand how money is defined.

According to economic experts, in order to consider anything as money, wealth or asset, it must possess the following three characteristics:

1. A medium of exchange

2. A unit of account

3. A store of value

1. Medium of Exchange

The most important task that must be carried out by money is that it should be a medium of exchange. It should be able to be utilized to purchase goods and services. As we saw in the beginning of the chapter that the barter system contained some deficiencies. For example, you wish to buy a chicken in exchange for saffron, but the person who has the chicken doesn't want saffron. He wants coal. Now you must set out in search of a person who has coal but is in need of saffron. Paper currency solves this dilemma.

By fulfilling the conditions of means of exchange, paper currency becomes a middle path, which can be used by anybody to make purchases. It provides an agreed-upon path for all.

This very property of medium of exchange is what makes cash more convenient than assets such as bonds, house or car etc.

By using paper currency instead of bartering, economic progress also takes place, the cost of transactions decreases, the skills and productivity of people increases, and a more equitable distribution of wealth can take place.

As an example, consider that I am a professor and I must deliver a lecture on bitcoin. In the barter system, I must go out in search for such a farmer who listens to my lecture in exchange for wheat for me to eat. Now you can imagine for yourself, how much time would be wasted in only this endeavor. How many farmers exist in the world who will wish to listen to a lecture on bitcoin. Either I will go hungry, or I will forget about bitcoin and turn to farming instead. Paper currency or cash solved such problems. It enabled each person to concentrate in doing what he or she does best. Money, after all, exists as a medium of exchange for us to fulfil our needs with.

I.   **Limited supply - scarcity**

For the durability of the value of money, it is important that its supply is scarce, otherwise it loses its value. This is what we witnessed with the coinage of the Roman empire, the 9th century paper currency of China and, more recently, with the Venezuelan bolivar.

Now, if your government just turns a blind eye and continues printing money day and night, its value will continue to fall. The supply of bitcoin, on the other hand, is limited, and only a total of 21 million of them will ever be issued.

II.   **Durability**

It is important for money not to be affected by the environment or weather. The more durable money is, the better it is. Like we saw that the age of a coin is 25 years and that of a 100-dollar note is about 15 years. Also, that you can fold your typical currency note about 8,000 times. Gold perfectly satisfies the condition of durability - neither does its rust or pale, nor does the heat, cold or rain affect it. Even animal leather, after treatment, works well and thus remained a medium of exchange for a long time. When salt was first discovered, its value was equivalent to that of gold. People would exchange 10 grammes of gold for 10 grammes of salt. There was a time when the Roman empire paid its soldiers in salt. The idiom 'nor worth a salt' has found its way in today's parlance. Bitcoin most certainly satisfies the condition of durability - no rain, heat or sunshine is likely to wear it.

III. **Divisibility**

Money must be divisible so that transactions of smaller value are possible. Whether a commodity costs 100 rupees, 50 or 25, you must be able to purchase it with convenience. Two 50 notes should be equal to one 100 note, and nobody should have any disagreement about it. One bitcoin can be distributed into a hundred million parts.

IV. **Portability**

It is important for a medium of exchange for it to be easily carried from one place to another. In small amounts, this is possible with gold also. But as the amount increases, the transfer of gold becomes more and more inconvenient. It is easy to transfer paper currency for most purposes, but there is a restriction on international transfers of cash - there are laws that discourage carrying cash over ten thousand dollars from one country to another. There exist taxes and large bank fees on large money transfers.

Bitcoin, on the other hand, can be transferred from one corner of the world to another within a matter of minutes, with just a click, and with incredibly low third-party charges.

V. **E. Unable to be copied**

You should easily be able to tell the difference between real and counterfeit money. In gold, this discrimination is done by the use of specialized tools. The common man can easily be deceived. This is possible in paper currency also, but as printing technology is evolving, counterfeiting money is getting more and more difficult.

Counterfeiting bitcoin is impossible - making copies of it is impossible from the mathematical and programmatic limitations.

VI. **Transferable**

Each unit must be the same as another of its kind, and nobody must have any objection if one is exchanged for another. Two notes of a thousand are equivalent in every respect. Two bars of gold of equivalent weight are similarly equivalent. Bitcoin is also transferable - one bitcoin is the same as another.

VII. **Widely accepted**

It is imperative for a medium of exchange to be readily and widely accepted by individuals and businesses, so that it could be used by anybody to conveniently make purchases. Bitcoin is gradually making its way in this respect.

2. Unit of account

By unit of account, we mean that standard by which the value of goods and services in an economy can be measured, and their prices determined. For example, we measure weight in kilograms or pounds, distances in kilometers or miles, electricity in volts, petrol or milk in liters or gallons, and so on. Likewise, the unit of account is a means to measure the value of consumable goods or economic activity. We will take another look at our previous example. Imagine that there exist only three commodities in the world: my bitcoin lectures, wheat and tomatoes. Thus, for all our transactions, we need only know three 'prices'. How many tomatoes in exchange for one bitcoin lecture? And how many kilograms of wheat in exchange for a kilogram of tomatoes? But if instead of 3 commodities in the economy, there were 10, this list of 'prices' would have gone up to 45.

$$\frac{N(N-1)}{2}$$

$$\frac{10(10-1)}{2} = \frac{90}{2} = 45$$

For 100 goods, 4,950 prices and for a 1,000 goods, 499,500 prices. If in a barter system, you entered a supermarket by mistake, the rest of your life would be spent only in reading the price-list. Money solves this problem by writing the price of each item in the prevailing currency. In countries where currencies are prone to extreme fluctuation on account of inflation, prices are written in dollars, even though transactions continue to take place in the local currency. A good example of this is in international airports around the world, where prices are mentioned in dollars. Also, when the list of the world's richest individuals is published, the estimate of their wealth is also made in dollars.

It is not necessary for a medium of exchange to also be a unit of account, but usually this is the case.

Because of fluctuation in value bitcoin is not a very good unit of account.

3. Store of value

The third important function of money is that it must serve as a store of value. When you receive your remuneration, you do not wish to spend it that very day. You have an assuredly fair idea of the amount of groceries you can purchase with it next week or next month. This function is common between currency and other assets such as property and bonds, etc.

Not all types of money function ideally as stores of value. If you keep your money in a mattress, it will lose at least 3% of its purchasing power each year on account of inflation. In about thirty years, it will be worth only half its original value.

In contrast, perhaps the value of gold or property would increase. Real estate and gold are assets that increase in value over time, but the liquidity - the ability to make immediate purchases - that currency gives is not present in these other assets.

There is no kind of money in the world that perfectly fulfils all three of these functions - medium of exchange, unit of account and store of value. Each type has its own pros and cons. Here, it is worth understanding that there is a difference between currency, wealth and income. By currency, we are referring to those notes or coins which are available to you. If somebody were to point a gun to your head and tell you to give up all your money, it is these notes and cash that you will empty your pockets and give up, rather than embark upon a lecture of the various kinds of 'money' in your ownership.

Wealth and assets refer to your bank balance, your property, car, bonds, stocks, and shares, etc. The United States has categorized cryptocurrency as asset / capital.

Income refers to the flow of money which is with respect to time periods. For example, if you tell me that your income is 100,000, I will ask whether it is daily, monthly or yearly. Moreover, an income statement does not tell us whether you have or don't have 100,000 in your possession at any point in time.

Then, there exist many further definitions and jargons of money. For example, in the jargon of banks, there is M1 money, M2 money (cash and bonds), fiat and digital cash, and so on.

The way we have defined money so far, scholars of Islam also agree to this. For example, Maulana Mufti Taqi Usmani sahib writes in his book *Islam and Modern Economy* "That which is used as a means of exchange, and which is a measure of value and which can be used to safeguard the value of wealth, that is 'money'".

The Maulana sheds light on interest in view of the historical Supreme Court ruling in respect to it, and says that money cannot directly fulfil human needs; rather it is used to purchase consumable goods and services.

In his collection of legal opinions (Fatawas), Sheikh Ibn Taimiah writes, "Dirhams and dinars are not desired as entities, but rather are a means of transactions."

Allam Ibn-ul-Qayyam said, "Money is not desired as an entity, but rather because of all that it can purchase. It is a means to attain goods. If money were to be categorized as goods, it will corrupt transactions between people."

Like Darwin's theory of evolution, money also evolves along with time and the changing needs of the time. In the last hundred years or so, without exaggeration, thousands of currencies came into existence, but today, only 193 of them remain. New epochs, new challenges, and new ways to deal with them. And it is thus that it will continue. The currency that is able to fulfil society's needs will survive, the rest will go extinct. One thing is for sure that were Darwin alive today, he would have preferred to take remuneration for his book 'On the Origin of Species' in bitcoin rather than in Pound Sterling.

~~~~~

Introduction to Blockchain

From birth to death - and perhaps even after death - man traverses a series of records and accounts. His entity, so to speak, and all the necessities and affairs associated with it, remain bound to some archive or the other. Were you to visualize an individual as one link in a chain of countless linked accounts, you would not be far from the truth. Imagine innumerable and unlimited accounts, all strung together. The facts recorded in each link are what man is; they serve as proof of his existence, and also provide him with what he needs from time to time. Trust me, this is no religious or philosophical wrangling I am indulging it; I am merely presenting that system according to which we exist, and which serves to be a practical prototype for the *blockchain*.

When we are born, the hospital issues a birth certificate, which is followed by a 'bay-form' usually from the office of the local councilor. Then, for the ultimate proof, a NADRA-issued Birth or Family Certificate is obtained. This voucher serves as a verification of your existence. Without this, your existence cannot legally be proved. Moving along, when you get your vaccinations, they are recorded in yet another register. Similarly, you buy a house, get your identity card or passport made, acquire your driver's license, bank account, arms license, marriage certificate, your children's birth certificates, school admissions, university degrees, and right down to your death, you receive some kind of certificate or the other - a proof of entry in some account or the other out there. I interpret this system as an invisible blockchain. Last but not least, consider our very Book of Deeds: isn't that too a register in which everything is *divinely* being taken account of.

Valuable goods, natural resources, national assets, population census - all have always required that the maintenance of their accurate record remains a possibility.

In 1944, following the Second World War, the Bretton Woods Conference took place and spawned institutions like the International Monetary Fund (IMF), World Bank (WB) and later, organizations such as the United Nations (UN) and World Trade Organization (WTO). The idea was to control all the resources of the world under a centralized system. All countries, big or small, and their helpless citizens, be they weak or powerful, all are brought under this central system where they proclaim to all and sundry their emancipation and their personal status. The truth is that ultimately, going through this central system, all their reserves and resources will come into the hands of a handful of individuals or institutions who in the name of policies, plans and procedures, will turn all free men into vassals.

Look around you and consider - isn't your entire life spliced with some central account-keeping mechanism or the other? Bank accounts, property documents, hospital records, identity documents, marriage license... the list goes on. What, then, is the problem with this? Why do we need an alternative system? Why must we forage for another possibility when everything seems to be going well?

There are three main problems with investing one's trust (or rather, blind trust) in a centralized system.

1. Exclusion

Under the pretext of competition, censorship or interest of the 'greater good', the system or those who run it can remove anybody from the system anytime that they want. By placing Pakistan on the Terrorism Watch List, limitations have been placed on the free movement of capital and goods. Similarly, Iran, Venezuela, Palestine, South Korea or any other nation for that matter which is not playing your tune is either excluded, or their inclusion made next to impossible. Paypal, for example, doesn't serve Pakistan. Over a billion people in the world do not possess the documents for their personal identification. From citizenship to government aid, from employment to medical access, they are unable to so much as prove their existence.

2. Dishonesty

People place their trust in an individual but he, in turn, indulges brazenly in injustice, plunder and corruption. People put their life savings in some institution and its board members squander it to their will. People pay taxes to their government, and instead of spending it on the welfare of the citizens, its representatives splurge it on luxuries.

3. Loss of records

What if somebody were to hack a central institution or bank and destroy all its records? What if a bank employee erroneously entered information into your account; or the records were obliterated by human error? What if a natural disaster, such as a fire, destroyed data files? In unfortunate situations like this, who then guarantees the rights of the victims?

The inequitable distribution of resources, illegitimate use of power, and unaccountable management of the system are additional reasons which continue to lend an air of mistrust. If one reflects on the previous century, one can sense that the greatest degradation in man happened in matters of trust. People have uniformly lost their trust, be it in institutions, governments, courts of law, relations, religions, leaders, or any other guarantors. The loss of collective trust and how to establish it between two or more parties in a centralized system is one of the foremost issues which have remained moot for the last 50 years.

Could we create such a register of accounts which can be read and written on so that all entries remain transparent? Could we remove the account of finances from the reins of any government, institution or individual? Why should any institution or individual take the responsibility of such a register? How is it possible that in an open account such as this, fraud and dishonesty can be impeded? Would such an account allow for changes?

In order to find answers to dozens of questions such as these, teams of researchers in mathematics, computer science, economics and psychology began churning the cogs. Like drops of rain, piecemeal, different parts of this new system began to emerge. Finally in 2008, a person with the fictional name *Satoshi Nakamoto* presented to the world a practical solution to this problem, which we know as **blockchain**.

What is blockchain and how does it work? Understanding this is a little difficult because one has to first become acquainted with all the ingredients that go into it. First, let us examine the qualities of this system and then gradually try to make sense of it with the help of examples.

Blockchain is an 'open', 'distributed' register which is accessible to everybody, in which everybody (under special conditions) can make entries, and which has been made secure using complex mathematics. This is the basic concept - I will offer a more comprehensive explanation of it in the next chapter after examining some examples.

As we have seen, in order to maintain records man has made use of registers or ledgers for centuries. At one time, these records were in the form of clay tablets, as we saw in Chapter 1. Other epochs made use of paper archives. In the modern world, records exist securely in computers in the form of bytes. Blockchain (a decentralized account) is a **distributer ledger** which keeps a chronological record of transactions. Each individual in the network possesses a complete copy of it. When some change occurs, or if some transaction takes place, each person updates his account. If somebody attempts to record a false transaction, the other people will reject it, for they will not have any record of that transaction in their accounts.

A common observation in marriage ceremonies is the medley of guests. Actually, all these guests serve to be a conscious blockchain who bear witness to the marriage. If at a future date, somebody were to claim marriage to this woman, all those guests will bear witness that this woman has already been wedded.

Consider the memorization of the Holy Quran. Each *hafiz* or memorizer is a **node** - each has a copy of the same public ledger, the Holy Quran, secured in his brain. Now, if in the future, some hare-brain, God forbid, attempts to bring forth a new verse (*ayah*), then the blockchain system of the *hufaz* will reject it and throw it out of the system. The blockchain we are examining works in exactly the same way.

Let us consider another example from our daily life. Abdullah is in need of money and calls his friend Jamshed on the phone and requests him for some. Jamshed, the kindly soul that he is, immediately opens his online account and transfers ten thousand rupees into Abdullah's account. Abdullah receives this amount in his bank in a matter of minutes.

Now, what went on behind his ordinary transaction? Of course, no actual currency or notes were physically transferred. When Jamshed opened his online account, he made a request to send ten thousand rupees. The computer system checked the availability of this amount of money in Jamshed's account. Had his account contained less than ten thousand rupees, the transaction would not have taken place. In this case, since his account did contain sufficient funds, ten thousand of them were deducted from his account and in Abdullah's account, ten thousand were increased. In this entire scenario, nothing more than a change of entry in the accounts took place. The only thing was that in order to transfer money between two individuals, a third party needed to be involved and trusted by both. Usually, this third party institution takes a fee in return for such services. Similar ordinary transactions between cities and countries, in fact, take even 10% of the amount and there is additionally a lag of 3 to 7 days. The amount would immediately be deducted from Jamshed's account but would take some time to be seen as an increase in Abdullah's.

When making use of a third party, in additional to service fees and time lags, all those issues prevail which we discussed earlier when talking about the problems of a centralized system. Additionally, the permission of the government and other institutions is also needed. Moreover, there is a further deduction in the transfer of foreign exchange. Add to this the probability of theft or human error and the fact that the convenience of transaction is also not particularly significant. It is as if we have kept all the eggs in a single basket - and that too, in somebody else's, which is commonly known as a bank.

Instead, can we not make a register of accounts among ourselves and keep entering our transactions in that? Ideally this can be achieved, but the practical problem of double-spending arises. This, Satoshi Nakamoto has brilliantly solved, and the solution is known as *blockchain*. We create a public ledger and keep a record of all transactions from the beginning to the end of time. If Abdullah goes ahead and gives five thousand to somebody else, then everybody knows that he had ten thousand and is therefore able to give five thousand, and also that those ten thousand came to him from Jamshed. Now, if hundreds and thousands of people are on this system, all their transactions will be entered and updated on this public register of the blockchain.

Each time that a page gets filled up with the transaction entries, all the people (*nodes*) will make use of the *hash function* to *seal* it and turn it into a *block*. They will then start working on the next block. The meaning of the *seal* is to establish that whatever was recorded on the page or block is correct and that no changes can ever be made to it. This is known as the *immutability* of the blockchain.

In layman terms, the *hash function* is a complex function of mathematics, somewhat like a machine, in which one can input whatever one wishes, and in answer, it will generate different answers of the same size. For example, if we enter the number '*4*', it may produce the answer '*dcbea*'.

4 ⟶ Hash Function ⟶ dcbea

Now, enter '26' and it will produce a different answer such as '94c8e'.

26 ⟶ Hash Function ⟶ 94c8e

Note that in the answer, in addition to alphabets, numbers can also be included. The hash function is a **one-way function**. This means that whenever we enter an input, the answer will be consistent. For example, the answer to '4' will always be 'dcbea'. However, there is no such way by which one can use the answer to arrive at the original number. And yes, it is easy to test it. If you know both '4' and 'dcbea', then with the help of this function, you can check to see in a matter of seconds whether the output is consistent with this input.

Now, if I were to say to you to tell me such an input which generates an output that begins with three zeros, how will you find this out?

Hash Function ⟶ 000 ? ⟶

The only way to find such an input is brute force. You keep entering one number after another as input and keep checking the outputs. Sometime or the other, the output that satisfies the condition will come up.

237 ⟶ Hash Function ⟶ 2bc7
C75ae ⟶ Hash Function ⟶ 9082
11802 ⟶ Hash Function ⟶ 09aef
.
.

72533 $\longrightarrow$ Hash Function $\longrightarrow$ 000ca

Aha! Got it! Now, this '*72533*' is your required number. Anybody can verify that if '*72533*' is entered as input, then the output contains three zeros in the beginning.

Now, we have to *seal* the page / block of our transaction. We will, for example, add up all the transactions that appear on the page (or for that matter, get a number in any other way). Now the relevant question is, which number should I put at the sum of the page such that there are three zeros in the beginning of the output.

For example, the sum of the page is '*20893*', so the question becomes:

20893 $\longrightarrow$ Hash Function $\longrightarrow$ 000... + ? ...

Now, we will try out luck with number after number. In due course, an appropriate number '*21191*' appears which satisfies the condition. So,

21191 + 20893 = 42084

42084 $\longrightarrow$ Hash Function $\longrightarrow$ 00078

This was our required number. Now with the help of this, we will *seal* our page or *block*.

This entire activity is known as *mining*, which, in the technical jargon of bitcoin, we call *proof of work*.

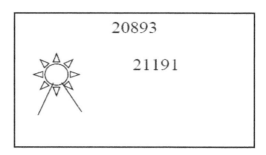

In addition to *sealing* the block, we have to attach it to the blockchain. Before joining each new block to the blockchain, a mathematical puzzle has to be solved, in which the previous page number, the new number which we are searching, and a new variable (*nonce*) are added, in order to arrive at the output.

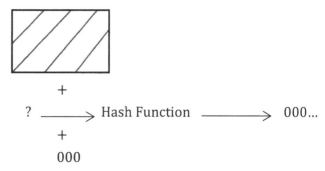

$$+$$
$$? \longrightarrow \text{Hash Function} \longrightarrow 000...$$
$$+$$
$$000$$

If some person were to attempt to add a fake block, he will not only have to join his current block, but also all the blocks that have ever been made in the blockchain, and then solve the mathematical puzzle. In order to accomplish this, he must gain access to 51% of all the networks in the world - otherwise, such a feat is not possible. This is known as *51% attack*.

At each new block, miners receive cryptocurrency as a reward. In the beginning, miners received 50 bitcoins, then 25 and currently 12.5. For the person with 51% power, it will be far more profitable to mine more blocks rather than destroy the entire system, after which nobody stands to gain anything. This is how the entire network remains honest and aboveboard.

There are three types of blockchain.

1. Public blockchain

As you have seen, bitcoin and Ethereum are examples of this. In public blockchains, anybody from anywhere can join the network whenever he wishes and leave whenever he wishes. In order to maintain the integrity in the nodes, they are given compensation for their work - new coins and transactions in the form of fees. The complex mathematical functions make it secure and hack-proof.

2. Private blockchain

Private blockchains are a company's internal public ledgers which only those can join whom the company allows. Here, since trust already exists between the people, since legal action can be taken in case of dishonesty, and because the true identity of the node is known, the act of mining is not very difficult. Consequently, the pace and capacity of such a block is thousands of times higher than that of a public blockchain.

For example, a bitcoin is able to complete a transaction every 7 seconds and a block is made every 10 minutes. In Ethereum, a block is made every 15 seconds. Paypal and credit card companies, in comparison, carry out hundreds of thousands of transactions per second. For such capacities in cryptocurrencies, *lighting networks* are being introduced.

3. Consortium blockchain

This blockchain is between a group of companies or partners and can only be joined by members. Here, rather than consensus, the rules of membership are applied.

To summarize, blockchain is a special kind of public ledger which is the basic underlying technology of cryptocurrencies such as bitcoin. This is a kind of data structure in which transaction in the form of blocks is joined to each other like links in a chain and with the help of the mathematical hash function. In the various kinds of blockchains, the public blockchain is the open kind. To join this, no kind of permission is required. Whoever wishes can join or leave it whenever they wish. In order to maintain trust between nodes that are strangers to each other, cryptocurrencies are awarded as recompense and discipline is made possible with the help of the different complex mathematical stages. Trust in private or closed blockchains, on the other hand, is usually made possible through the company's policies and agreements. Thus, in such blockchains, cryptocurrency is not given as reward. All the rest of the phases, such as consensus and voting, for example, are more or less the same.

As we discovered in the first chapter, the origins and forms of money have varied much - from salt to animal skin, from the *rai* stone to tobacco. If something had access and demand, it was used by way of currency. Along with the internet was born digital currency as well. In 1882, David Chaum presented the ***blind signature*** and ***e-cash***. In 1997, Adam Back came up with ***Hash Cash***; in 1990 Wei Dai with ***B-Money***; in 1998 Nick Szabo with ***Bit-Gold***; and in 2004 Hal Finney with ***Reusable Proof of Work RPOW***. These theories and inventions culminated in 2008 with Satoshi Nakamoto introducing the world to ***Bitcoin***.

Currently, it is unlikely that there exists any large bank in the world that is not studying the blockchain in some form or another. In 2015, IBM in collaboration with Linux Foundation, started the ***Hyper Ledger Fabric*** project which, to date, has been brought into use by hundreds of companies. With investment of billions, over 2,500 patents and more than 800 crypto assets, blockchain is about to bring the kind of changes to the economic system which email brought to the postal system and cellphones to the landline communication system.

Foresight is in assimilating this technology to greater and greater extent in the coming years and making its effective uses a reality. According to one survey, in 2020 the world will need at least 500,000 blockchain developers. Currently, there are not even 5,000. If you were to invest yourself in this today, your employment and business prospects in the future are full of promise.

In the following chapter, we will explore some technical and practical aspects.

~~~~~

Blockchain – Technical Assessment, Architecture and Need

Keeping the previous discussion in mind, a comprehensive and technical definition of a blockchain would be something like this:

"Blockchain is a computer's ***peer-to-peer***, ***decentralized*** and ***distributed*** public ledger which keeps a complete, secure and unchangeable record of a forthcoming transaction."

Blockchain makes transactions possible in such an environment where there is not only little trust between people, institutions or devices, but rather a complete lack of it. For security, blockchain makes use of the complex mathematical algorithms of cryptography and in order to keep the participating nodes honest, also gives them both rewards and punishments. This record is chronologically maintained - along with the transaction, the time at which the transaction took place is also recorded. A transaction entered in the blockchain can never be changed. The entry recorded in a register tells the exact time of the transaction, thus providing a solution to the problem of double-spending. Furthermore, a complete record of the fund is available: when did it come into existence, when and where it was spent and who is the current owner of it.

Let's try to simulate the addition of a block of bitcoin to the blockchain in order to see what is technically taking place during this process. Imagine that we have downloaded the complete bitcoin blockchain from the public system. Our computer node intends to add a new block to it. The last and most recent block is number '349'. Ours will be number '350'.

One block contains the complete record of all the transactions that occurred during the previous ten minutes. As soon as some transaction takes place, the blockchain system broadcasts it to all the nodes in the system. Each node checks whether this was in fact a valid transaction or not, i.e. they check for double-spending. Then they pass it though the cryptographic **hash function** and add it to the block. Bitcoin uses a hash function called SHA-256. Its basic concept is what we have already seen in the previous chapter. For further information, you may consult the hash function page on the Block Geeks website[40]. Now, after passing through the cryptographic hash, the final transaction received from the nodes becomes a part of the block and is stored with the help of the **Merkle tree**. If any change were to be brought to any transaction, the entire Merkle tree would have to be processed all over again.

Now, before including the **Merkle root** in the blockchain, we will find out the hash of the header of the block in which we must solve the puzzle with the nonce value. In order to do this, with the help of the header of the previous block '349', the Merkle root and the nonce value, we will search for that **seal** which will be used in block '350'. As soon as this mathematical puzzle gets solved, we will broadcast the previous block's header hash, the Merkle root, the nonce value and the newly obtained number on the network. All the nodes will check these values, and if they prove to be correct, they will add the new block '350' to the blockchain. The miner will then receive bitcoins as reward. This entire process of blockchain block composition can be seen visually in figures below.

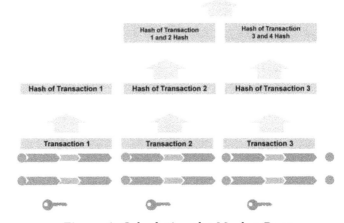

Figure 1: Calculating the Market Root

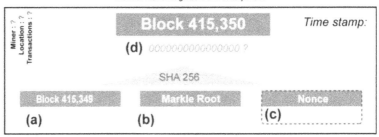

Figure 2: Mining a Block

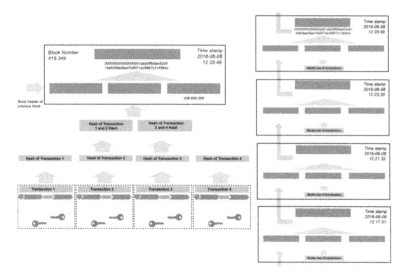

Figure 3: Bitcoin Visualization

From the software point of view, we can divide the blockchain architecture in three parts:

1. Protocol layer,
2. Network layer, and
3. Application layer

Protocol Layer: The protocol layer tells us which programming language and computing recourses we are using, how the nodes will be added in the system, how the consensus will take place, how the value or funds will be transferred, and how the reward will be given. It also tells us which type of blockchain we are using – permissionless (public) or permissioned (private) – and what are the functionality, design, programming and speed specifications one should consider. It is wise to look for available team skills, developers' pool and if such a pool is available through open-source communities. The main stakeholders in this layer are academia and developers. Where the former is interested in adding research and knowledge in the system for recognition, the latter is bound to develop technical frameworks and protocols for intellectual challenge and career prospects.

Network Layer: The network layer tells us how the mutual relations within the system will happen, i.e. how will the miners, nodes, data and applications communicate with each other. The relevant issues here are: who runs the node, who has the read/write access, what is the calculation complexity and requirements for a given node, how we are storing data, what are the requirements for data storage, archiving and network throughput, how technology integration will take place and how to deal with government regulation and standard specification at each step. This middle layer is the most complex layer of the blockchain architecture. The main stakeholders include miners, standard formation bodies, crypto-exchanges and traders. Miners would validate the transaction for financial gain, standard formation bodies would target their own objectives through industry goals and frameworks, and exchange and traders would provide access to value tokens to speculate prices for monetary gains.

Application Layer: The application layer tells us which applications or clients will be able to operate on this network and what the laws and conditions of their system will be. Who are the end users? How the user journey will takes place and what are the implications of user experience and design? How will the offering cater for users' behavior and day-to-day business and what changes are needed for business logic or within organizational hierarchy to implement a given use case? The prime stakeholders for this layer are consumers, investors and venture funds, corporates and institutions, entrepreneurs and startups. Entrepreneurs would build new use cases to increase business and profits, corporates will use technology for efficiency and optimization, consumers will use the products for better services, features and cost optimization and investors would fuel the growth for long-term financial gains.

The following are the six fundamental characteristics of the blockchain system. It is:

- distributed,
- encrypted with the help of cryptography,
- keeps a complete history,
- is immutable,
- is public, and
- for value transfer, makes use of some currency or value token or the other

If you wish to find out whether or not your system is capable of being taken to a blockchain, or whether or not you should dispense with your current system and migrate to the blockchain, then ask yourself the following five questions. If you answer yes to all of them, then certainly the use of blockchain will be greatly beneficial to you.

1. Is there such a process which can be predicted and has to be continually repeated for long time (instead of one time) occurrence that can easily be automated instead?

2. Are there many participants/stakeholders in your system or value chain?

3. Do you receive data in various formats and at different times from a range of individuals or institutions? Does the role of reconciliation of data depend on one or a number of parties?

4. Is there any value transfer other than financial, such as music, arts, legal documents, votes, etc.?

5. Is it necessary for you to keep a complete history of the transaction (immutable record) and to curtail the possibility of altering it?

If your system is in need of these attributes, then blockchain can present an ideal solution for you. Contrary to popular belief, blockchain is not a silver bullet to solve everything under the sun. There are many factors to consider when deciding the technical application of a blockchain for a given use case. One such factor is: where will the application data reside? Database technology and centralized client-server architecture has considerably matured over decades and you may find the traditional database a better fit over blockchain if the application performance is important, the availability of large number of trained developers is required, if the data is highly confidential or sensitive to share on a public ledger, if you do not need a chronological tally of the data being recorded, if ease of maintenance is something you look for, if the software production cycle is agile, where the business and technical logic is expected to change frequently or when maintaining the centralized control (data sovereignty) is necessary. However, blockchain will be a better solution if the application requires transparency and public validation, extreme fault tolerance, infinite scalability, complete history of data and immutability, and importantly, the condition that no single authority should be entrusted with the data.

~~~~~

Initial Coin Offering (ICO)

To start any business or enterprise, capital is needed. Traditionally, there are several ways to acquire this capital. For example:

1.   You can invest your savings (if you have any)

2.   You can sell some of your assets such as jewelry or vehicle, etc.

3.   You can borrow money from family or friends

4.   You can borrow money on interest from a bank

5.   You can borrow money from institutions against shares in the company or as convertible notes (amount needs to be paid back within a prescribed time with agreed-upon interest, or it will be automatically converted to the company's shares at a discounted price). Each shareholder is now entitled to part-ownership of your company to the extent of his shares. The majority shareholders can even determine your salary. If more than 50% of the shareholders decide to remove you from the company ownership, they are very capable of doing even that. Moreover, you have to register all these concerns with the Security Exchange Commission (SEC) and you are liable to abide by your country's laws and rules of various government institutions. All this naturally makes the process somewhat cumbersome.

6.   You can get funds from the public by carrying out an IPO. IPOs need an underwriter (investment bank) to facilitate the process and to meet the statuary requirements by the Security and Exchange Commission (SEC).

All these tasks require a lot of time for thinking, planning, taking care of regulatory affairs, satisfying government requirements and proving that you are, indeed, a trustworthy person spearheading a venture that deserves to be funded.

In recent years, crowd funding has challenged these age-old practices by creating a way to ask for funds directly from common people all over the world. By proving the details of your company or venture, the credentials of your team and further technical details on websites such as KickStarter or GoFundMe, you can appeal for funds from people all over the world. Most of these funds are in the form of donations; the donor gets nothing out of it and supports your work by way or charity. In some cases, at the completion of project, the donor can either claim benefits such as samples of your product, or their funds back, according to pre-decided agreements. The company usually deducts a commission of between 10-15% of these funds before returning them. If you are unable to interest a significant number of people to fund you, or the funding target fails to be achieved, then all the funds will be returned to the respective donors and you will gain nothing. Sites like GoFundMe, KickStarter and LaunchGood have raised over 5 billion dollars for various campaigns and projects that users have posted on their sites. Even charity organizations like Kiva are following trend and opening up funding avenues for individual needs.

Initial Coin Offering (ICO) is actually a modern take on the above-mentioned crowd funding practice – it is a method of raising funds used by cryptocurrency and blockchain based startups. The entire process is the same, with the difference that all of it is done on blockchain and the funds received are in cryptocurrency. In return, you give the donor some tokens of your project or company. The new native currency created by the startup is sold to investors against Bitcoin or Ethereum. In contrast to traditional crowd funding, ICOs offer donors the prospect of increase in value of the tokens so that they can earn a profit solely by virtue of donating. Investors buy the coins or tokens of a new company in the hope that its price will increase following the launch. For example, the price of Ethereum at ICO was 25 cents, and it is now running at around $500 per coin. The world has never before seen profit margins such as these. Most of the startups in ICOs sell their coins as pre-sale tokens or donations to avoid legal and regulatory authorities. The native tokens are then listed on private crypto exchanges like Binance, etc. for further trading after the successful ICO.

Contrary to regular funding methods with financial and audit reports, ICOs start with a simple 'whitepaper' explaining the technology, total number of tokens, percentage of tokens being offered on sale, the percentage that founders and developers will get, and the funds that will be kept separate for further extension of the platform or technology. It also details the goals, mission and timelines of the project, in addition to how long the ICO will run and what kinds of cryptocurrencies will be accepted. If the funds raised do not meet the minimum criteria for ICO funding, all funds will be returned to investors and the ICO will be deemed unsuccessful. If the funds raised are above the required maximum limit, the extra funds will also be returned.

There are 3 basic types of tokens issued by the company:

1. Coins

Each project has its own native currency. For example, when Ethereum ran its ICO, Ethereum was valued at 40 cents. From USD 0.4, it reached a value of USD 1,300 in due course - about a 4,000 times profit!

2. Utility tokens

These are units of service which can be used at a later date. For example, you participate in a school's ICO, and then later, in exchange for these tokens, you can get your children schooled at that institution. There are many examples of this in the music and arts industry.

3. Security tokens

These are exactly like traditional company shares - possession of these makes you a part owner of the company. For these, it is necessary to be registered at the SEC. In order to find out which token comes in the domain of SEC, the United States SEC has laid down the conditions of Howey Test. If any kind of money is used in the purchase of security tokens, the money has been given to some company and the donor stands to claim a profit solely by investing and without any hard work, then this process is known as Security and on this, all the rules of SEC stand to apply.

ICOs do also fail, plummeting the value of its token to zero. It is highly advisable to understand the characteristics of a good ICO before investing in such a venture. The project should be related to crytocurrency and blockchain, it should have a detailed whitepaper, and the management and technical team should be sound with respect to skills, credentials and past success in the domain or related domain of their intended project. Moreover, the distribution of funds in question should be transparent (coin allocation), and the total ask-for amount should be between 2 million to 10 million dollars. The ICO should also have the direct application of its token soon after the ICO (the use case), and you should be able to talk to and reach the founders with ease.

There have also, unfortunately, been a couple of hacking incidents where hackers were able to steal large amounts of ICO-based money from startups – recently, DAO, Ethereum and a couple of exchanges. More incidents like this are likely to tighten regulations and make them harder to work with for the foreseeable future. We need a technologically superior system that would be compatible with regularity affairs , or create a regulatory sandbox to experiment with new models of funding while protecting the resources and money for entrepreneurs, investors and public at large.

In order not to dampen the spirit around ICOs, it is worth looking at some ICO success stories. In 2013, an ICO by the name of NXT ran from 28 September to 8 November of that year. Twenty-one bitcoins were collected from 73 investors which were collectively worth USD 14,000. In only a few years, the profits gained by these 73 investors was 200,000 %. The Ethereum ICO ran from 20 July 2014 to 2 September 2014 (about 42 days) and collected about 21,500 coins which would be valued today at USD 18 million. This ICO earned its investors a 4,000% profit. The ICO of LISK ran from 22 February to 21 March 2016. USD 5.7 million was collected and the profit was 138%. The ICO of Waves was USD 16 million and that of DAO was USD 160 million. To date, there have been over a thousand ICOs which have done business of over USD 10 billion. In light of the growing popularity of ICOs, you can call them the security shares of the future.

Among prospective tokens, those worthy of mention are Human-IQ (which helps the poor gain inclusion in the international economic system), Eternity (where smart contracts will be able to work with live data), and others such as Internet of Coins, Cosmos, Blue Frontiers, Gnosis, Etherex and Akasha. These ICOs are expected to garner significant profit through business. Within ICOs as well, many further innovation are being introduced. IBO (Initial Bounty Offering) is an example, where initial developers of the project are given IBO tokens when they complete their share of the work. On average, an ICO is able to collect USD 12.7 million and on average, the percentage of profit expected is 12.8 times.

With the help of the Ethereum platform and the ERC20 token standard, anybody can issue their own tokens in a matter of hours. Before getting involved in an ICO, it is advisable to check the local laws, lest in your ignorance you get embroiled in legal complexities. China, for example, has completely banned ICOs and the US has applied many laws. Nowadays, regulations are the biggest threat to ICOs. It is wise to check if the prospective ICO would clear the Howey Test – "a person invests his money in a common enterprise and is led to expect profits solely from the efforts of the promoter or a third party ." If the ICO can be classified as a security as per the Howey Test, it clearly means that the investor and the startup both have to follow SEC guidelines and regulations in the process, or risk losing their enterprise and money.

There exist many websites, such as Token Foundry , which can help you in launching your ICO. For further information, explore websites such as Token Market , ICO List , Smith & Crown , ICO Bench , ICO Countdown , ICO Rating and Crypto Compare , to name a few.

~~~~~

Legal Compliance Framework and Considerations for an ICO

Family-owned businesses contribute a significant share to a country's GDP and to promote them is a desirable outcome for Small and Medium Enterprise Development authorities of any country. ICO has raised $ 6.3 billion in 2018 so far[41], while the overall funding in ICOs has touched $ 20 billion[42] – far ahead of any combined funding for a new technology in the history of the world. It offers an immense and timely opportunity to raise funds and scale up businesses.

At the same time, we need to be conscious that the ICO is not crossing any ethical boundaries of the society it operates in. For example, the money should not be used for or come from ignoble businesses like pornography, Darknet, ransom, killing, drugs or sex trafficking. Further, it should not be used with any business involving crimes, illicit use and commonly overlooked societal ills like cyber-bullying, cyber-stalking, revenge porn, child pornography, data ransom, kidnapping ransom, identity theft, or to support any hostile acts against nations.

Blockchain is borderless, nations are not, and therefore we should be very careful about legal compliance when our ICO is seeking funds from multiple geographies. Following is the list of nine compliance categories one should be aware of before launching an ICO.

1. **Legal Framework:** Based on the nature and location of your ICO and prospective investors, which legal bodies and frameworks does one need to adhere to? Securities and Exchange Commission (SEC), the Commodity Futures and Exchange Commission (CFTC), the Internal Revenue Service (IRS), and the Financial Crimes Enforcement Network (FinCEN)[43] are a few relevant institutions. Confirming the legal framework will guide us towards compliance for each statuary authority and its respective regulations[44].

2.   **Legal Status:** Are you planning to launch the ICO in the US and Europe? If so, you would like to know the legal status it will fall into in the US[45] and Europe. Please confirm it with the SEC framework for ICOs[46] in the US and European Union Law[47]. European Union has recently issued several warnings[48] for ICO investment and one should ensure the compliance for ICO. Will it be considered as a security[49] (or investment contract under standards established by the U.S. Supreme Court in SEC v. W.J. Howey Co[50].) or a token? Does it pass the Howey Test in the US[51] (a token is a security when there is an investment in a common enterprise with an expectation of profits from the efforts of others) or could it be classified as a utility token[52]? Can it be classified for private sale under Rule 506(b) of Regulation D[53] or for general solicitation under Rule 506 (C)[54]? How will it affect the sale of tokens in the secondary markets? Can the token tradability be classified as a commodity under US Commodity & Exchange Act[55]? Which legal framework would be applicable to the exchange facilitating the ICO; does it fall under the US Exchange Act[56] or European Securities and Market Authority (ESMA)[57]? Here is a good resource to look for the comparison of the two[58]. Does it prohibit US and EU residents to participate in the ICO? Would it make it unlawful for the exchange (directly or indirectly) to conduct these transactions? How would the legal status differ under UK's Financial Conduct Authority (FCA) framework[59]? How does our ICO measure against the Simple Agreement for Future Tokens (SAFT) framework[60] and what we can change to make sure regarding the compliance? Does it fall into Anti-Fraud SEC Rule 10b-5[61]? Knowing the legal framework would help us craft a safe compliance strategy.

3.   **Agent/Partnership**: Who is in our sales team? What are their backgrounds and are they under investigation by SEC for any past endeavors? Does it affect our ability and credibility to launch our ICO with them? Does their work fall under Investment Advisor's Act of 1940[62]? Does it make us liable for any of their past wrong-doings? Knowing the nature and responsibilities for engaging with the sales team

will allow us to gauge the efforts and resources we need to commit before making the decision.

4.   Jurisdiction: Where is the corporate office located? How would it affect our ability to raise funds from US and European Union citizens? Do we need to register a satellite office in the US and Europe as well or can we raise the funds without a local physical presence? In case of dispute or lawsuits, which country's law will be followed? Do we need to deal with each case respective of its origin? Knowing the real geo-spatial boundaries and applicable regulations would help us form the ICO launch strategy while making sure of the complete geographical-legal compliance.

5.   Sanity Check on Funds Distribution: Please review your white paper and see if the post-ICO funds distribution is legal – the amount of tokens you will give to founders, advisors, developers, bounty hunters, and investors. Do you have to change the percentages to comply with the US or European Law or is it open to decide as you will? Can you peg the token value to a FIAT for volatility control? Knowing the fairness of funds distribution on legal grounds will help you market it with confidence.

6.   Money Transfers and Regulations Arbitrage: How do you comply with AML/CTF/KYC (Anti-Money Laundering, Counter-Terrorism-Financing, and Know Your Customers) laws on each state and jurisdiction you raise the funds from? As the US and the EU have different compliance laws, you may like to give flexibility to your investors wherever it is available. How do you comply with the US Bank Secrecy Act (BSA)[63]? Or do you need to acquire a money transmitter license[64]? Knowing the answer to these questions will save you legal troubles in respective geographies and help you avoid big legal battles for money laundering and counter-terrorism.

7.   Taxation: IRS defines tokens as "property" and thus it is taxable for the party selling it. How does it affect the legality of your ICO? How much money do you owe to IRS, being a non-US company? How will the newly crafted

Cryptocurrency Tax Fairness Act of 2017 bill[65], if passed, change the situation? Knowing your tax liabilities will help you manage the funds better.

8.   **Personal Identifiable Information (PII):** Which laws do you need to comply with for investors' privacy, as you are taking personal and financial details of your investors? Which security guidelines and framework should you use for international transactions and to guarantee the anonymity of your investors (especially if they are from outside the US and EU)? Knowing the underlying dynamics of security PII will help you plan a better security strategy for your ICO and respective investors' data.

9.   **Customer Engagement Model**: You also need a legal review of your "Terms and Agreement" that is available on your website. You need to make sure it reflects your compliance and standards for the cross-border fund-raising and money transfers. Knowing the legal consequences of customers' engagement model will help you improve the user experience and to comply with the legalities of forming a legal contract online.

Based on this legal compliance framework, one should get an overall idea of where one stands for legal compliance. It also informs one of the possible corrective measures one can take to change the trajectory towards legal compliance. How to avoid falling into regulation arbitrage and AML/KYC/CTF legal traps, for example? This framework will come handy. You need to add your local country laws in this list to make sure you are not risking non-compliance.

~~~~~

Smart Contracts

Smart contracts – first coined by Nick Szabo in 1994[66] – are digital protocols to enforce performance, and verify and negotiate the contract among two or more parties. It is an algorithmic way of carrying out transactions and deals between two or more parties, where the trust, consensus, consequences and resulting payments will be decided by the smart contract on the basis of pre-agreed conditions.

There are quite a few types of smart contracts. For example, one that is between two or more parties and will have its own interpretation of the state of affairs. Another type is more detailed and it would also interpret the algorithmic rules into Ricardian contract that a human can understand.

Smart contracts usually work with blockchain. If it is on blockchain, then it has to use the consensus protocol to "verify" the state of affairs or be dependent on some validators and reporters to confirm and report the end results before it triggers the ending set of commands like making payments. To be on blockchain, it would also need to use "Value Tokens" to incentivize the validators, reporters and nodes who are working on consensus.

Smart Contract on a permissioned blockchain or simply on any DLT (Distributed Ledger Technology) without a blockchain would act like a normal computer program that would follow the rules, have its own criteria to measure the success of events and will follow the rest of the program. In that case, it cannot "enforce" its condition and thus risks losing the charm of "smart contract" altogether. It does not need a consensus protocol or the value tokens to be shared by nodes/validators/reporters.

For example, smart contract between two IoT devices in a controlled, trusted environment may not need blockchain. Or, for example, if someone likes a certain percentage (say 0.02%) of their pay to go to their kid's account/wallet as his/her pocket money, there is no need to place it on public ledger.

Smart contract on permissioned blockchain would offer cost effectiveness and fast processing but would fall behind in the political landscape from adoption to acceptability and from standardization to liability.

There are quite a few properties of smart contracts that we should care about, such as:

1.   **Immutability:** To human is err, and when smart contracts interact with humans, mistakes can happen for which we should have a recourse

2.   **Security:** It is good to have features, but if you type one thing wrong you can lose your money irrevocably. On the other side, the bad guys like hackers and malicious users have all the time in the world to scan the complete chain to find and exploit any vulnerability.

3.   **Confidentiality:** There is always this showing-too-much phenomenon in the name of transparency, which may breach confidentiality.

4.   **Quality of Data:** Smart contracts need a secure bridge with external data and with machine and human oracles.

5.   **Language:** Which language is the smart contract designed in? How is the language evolving and how would it affect the future interaction of smart contract if there are any inherent changes in its structure and design?

6.   **Clients:** Which client to use and work with – Geth, Parity, Claymore? Which one is more secure, easily accessible and cost effective?

7.   **Frameworks:** Which framework is the smart contract using? Meteor, Maven, Truffle, Embark, Zeppelin? What are the security, accessibility and cost trade-offs?

8.

9. **Best Practices:** Smart Contract should follow the best practices of the business domain it is working in or risk losing its credibility, functions and money

10. **Storage:** Is it going to store all the data on blockchain itself or can it use some decentralized storage like Swarm or IPFS?

11. **Costs:** Last but not least, what are the costs associated with the smart contract and what would it take to keep it running?

~~~~~

How to Become a Blockchain Developer

Blockchain, Crypto-Currencies, Ethereum, Smart Contracts and ICOs have become the most frequently used words in computer science, FinTech and investment circles these days. Everyone likes to have skin in the game—to invest, earn/lose, re-invest and become a millionaire before anyone else would know it.

Blockchain is doing to startups & businesses (in general) and FinTech (in particular) what Email has done to post-office mails, mobile phones to landlines, Netflix to Blockbusters, Amazon to RadioShack, and what Digital pictures have done to Kodak.

It is the era of blockchain and distributed ledger technology—it is not the question of if and when you will realize it, it is how much you lose while taking the time to come to that realization.

William Mougayar mentioned in his book Business of Blockchain[67] that there are 5,000 blockchain developers in the world (mid-2016); compare this with 9 million Java developers and 18.5 million software developers worldwide[68]. According to the CEO of Pantera Capital[69], cryptocurrencies will hit the $40 trillion market cap. ComputerWorld[70] says the median salary of a blockchain developer is $158,000/year and the hourly rate is $150/hour. UpWork has seen 3500% increase[71] in the demand of blockchain skills over the year and according to TechCrunch[72] there is only one candidate available for 14 blockchain jobs today. There is a job for every aspect of the blockchain ecosystem, there is a job if you know how to code smart contracts, there is a job for cryptography experts, there is a job for consensus developers, there is a job for Ripple suit of applications, and there is a job for IBM's Hyperledger Fabric. It doesn't matter which part of this ecosystem you work in, there is a job available (right now) for you. Portals like Blocktribe[73] are dedicated to blockchain related jobs only. There are 5,000+ blockchain startups, and ICOs have raised close to $7 billion worldwide. The world would need half a million blockchain developers in the next five years. The question is what you can do to secure a job and make your dreams come true, and how you can become someone that would qualify for these half a million jobs worldwide.

There is a lot of confusion and misrepresentation out there when it comes to defining the blockchain. Here is my very brief and simple blockchain definition that almost everyone can agree upon:

"Blockchain is a peer-to-peer, decentralized, distributed ledger that permanently and chronologically records and guarantees an immutable, unalterable, trustworthy transaction (of money or any valuable asset) in a trust-less environment through consensus protocol secured by cryptography with economically incentivized participation."

Blockchain is an immutable, open, secure, and transparent shared ledger that anyone can voluntarily join and leave at will. It has two broad types: Public (with open participation incentivized and punished by consensus protocol) and Private (with a consortium or private businesses' vetted membership and enforcement of laws and regulations in place). Compared to centralized structures, blockchain saves time, removes cost, reduces risk and increases trust.

The question is, what one can do to become a good blockchain developer if he/she cannot afford or fails to get selected for competitive and expensive programs? What can someone from a developing country like Pakistan do to improve his/her chances of getting hired in this important field or even try to use these advanced skills to improve their surroundings, communities, and countries?

Here is a cheat sheet for becoming a good Blockchain Developer (almost) for free:

1. Start by watching Neha Narula's Ted talk on the Future of Money[74]

2. Don Tapscott's talk on how blockchain is changing money and business should be your next click[75]

3. Let's take a step back to find out why we have stopped trusting institutions by Rachel Botsman[76] and the role of middlemen by BCG[77]

4. Have a look at the future of Branded Money with Paul Kemp[78]

5. Mark Schwartz sheds light on Potential of Blockchain[79]

6. We will end our visual journey with Bettina Warburg's talk on Radical Transformation by Blockchain[80]

7. HBR article – The Truth about Blockchain[81] should be your first read in this journey

8. Make sure to bookmark these organizations for regular updates and to find out where the industry is heading— Digital Currency Initiative at MIT[82], Oxford Blockchain Network[83], Digital Chamber of Commerce[84], R3[85], Hyperledger[86], ConSenSys[87] and Blockchain Research Institute[88]

9. There are couple of books to get started and most of these are available for free to download: Blockchain for Dummies[89], Mastering Blockchain 1st Edition[90], A Gentle Introduction to Blockchain Technology[91], Mastering Bitcoin by Andreas M. Antonopoulos[92], Virtual Currency: the Bitcoin Manual by Lachlan Roy[93],

10. There are hundreds of courses and workshops are available out there to teach you crypto-currencies, blockchain and related technologies. There is a Byte Academy's 14-week on-site program in New York that costs $10,000, there is Oxford Blockchain Strategy Program for around $3,000, there is ConSenSys developers program for $1,000 and even a complete Masters ($12,000) and Ph.D. program in Blockchain by University of Nicosia. There are also quite a few specialized course providers, such as B9Lab, BitDegree, Udemy and Lynda. However my personal favorite is BlockGeeks; it should be your first stop. It is the best resource out there and offers courses from the basics of blockchain to ERC20 tokens and from Segwit to Smart Contracts. You can learn it all for under $200 a year.

No one can stop you if you wish to become a blockchain developer, it will take around a year, a few hundred dollars, a firm commitment, a lot of patience and heavy programming practice to become one. Once you go through all or some of it, you can practice at GitCoin[94] to see how good you can code and get paid for your work. You can also submit your profile at CrossOver and get a remote job for $100,000/year. Even if you complete half of it, send me a note and I will have something ready for you.

The ball is in your court; it does not matter where you are and how much you can afford, if you want to make at least four times higher than the average income in your country, this is the way to do it, at least for the next ten years.

~~~~~

Cryptocurrencies and Natural Selection

From Aristotle's Scala Naturae – the chain of being – to Adam Smith's invisible hand, the dynamics and evolution of money has always been the invisible chain of transactions and transfers among the human populace. Let's dive deeper to find out how natural the ideological revolution and prophecy of blockchain is to human life.

Darwinian evolution comprises of three steps: **Variation** – the variants in a new generation doesn't need to be directed, they can be as blind and random as can be. **Selection** – a criterion to judge the best fit for the environment (this providing direction), and **Inheritance** – the retention of key traits of the previous generation for a stable cumulative capability of the species.

Natural selection in biology refers to the different rates of survival and reproduction, due to differences of traits, properties, behavior and products of behavior of individual organisms. When individuals of a species reproduce, regardless if it happens by splitting (for example in microbes) or by combining DNA of two individuals (sexual reproduction, like in most mammals, birds, etc.), there is always a slight chance of a random mutation happening and leading to the resulting individual(s) having new or changed traits, which their "parents" did not have. In some cases, these traits (or changes to them) happen to improve the chances of those individuals who have them to survive and/or reproduce in their current environment, which increases the chance of these traits to be passed on to the offspring. Over time, the traits which enable higher rates of survival / reproduction become prevalent, while "competing" traits subside. As the ability of a trait to enable higher survival / reproduction rate depends on the environment (for example, thick fur might be beneficial in a cold climate, but would be a disadvantage in a hot climate), when individuals of the same species migrate to different environments, they develop different traits over generations. There is no particular moment when a new species is "born" – every offspring belongs to the same species as their parents, yet over a sufficiently long timeframe, the difference in various traits between individuals living in different environments becomes so big, that they cannot be considered the same species anymore[95].

There is a Darwinian struggle for survival, between the current cryptocurrency heavyweights. This is a new paradigm that requires money to be decentralized or smart (programmable). Cryptocurrencies possess these traits, gold and fiat currencies do not. Cryptocurrencies have added heightened competition. All currencies are in a state of hyper-evolution. Growing distrust in centralized entities has encouraged many to consider alternative stores of value. Sovereignty, once a trait necessary for the survival of a currency, has fallen out of favor. Centralized failures have created growing awareness that a decentralized world is possible. Historically, the existence and survival of any entity, be it plant, animal, corporation, or currency is subject to the laws of natural selection. However, there have been several mass-extinction events during the history of life. Such an event happens when the environment changes so drastically and/or so rapidly, that most of the species existing at that time fail to adapt quickly enough and are annihilated. An example of such an event is an asteroid hitting Earth, which made the dinosaurs go extinct. Fiat financial system's mass-extinction event has already occurred. It began with the birth of the Internet, peer-to-peer technological revolution and the 2008 financial crisis. Fiat is sliding into irrelevancy. The internet of money (cryptocurrencies led by Bitcoin) and the Internet-of-Things (IoT) era has already begun. During this period, fiat may very well become extinct and be replaced by cryptocurrencies. The average life of a fiat currency is 27 years. The main reasons for the increasing irrelevancy of fiat currencies are monetary reforms, hyperinflation, wars, and changing geopolitical climates (for example, countries declaring independence). Even without failure, all fiat currencies continually lose value, which was not the case with most commodity-based currencies.

As easy accessibility is needed for currencies to gain widespread acceptance, cryptocurrencies currently still use the on-ramps interacting with the legacy currency systems. While everyone can acquire cryptocurrencies simply by accepting them as payment for their work, goods, or services, a lot of people still choose to use exchanges for purchasing (and selling) cryptocurrencies. These third-party institutions safeguard private keys and facilitate trades. In a way, they benefited from centralization – governments' acceptance enabled entrepreneurship and investor confidence. Long term, exchanges, especially centralized ones, are not needed at all. Fully decentralized exchanges already exist (not only crypto-to-crypto, but fiat-to-crypto as well), for example Bisq[96].

Markets are not constant – the only constant is fluctuation and change. Market participants must therefore also adapt. While several years ago, the most popular cryptocurrency to be used in Darknet markets has been Bitcoin, while recently Monero has become the currency of choice on the Darknet, as it has much better anonymity / privacy features than Bitcoin[97].

The ability to adapt should not be equated to being easily changeable. Sometimes, the ability of individuals or species to remain unchanged and uninfluenced by outside factors are actually the best adapted to the environment, especially if the environment, and the influencing factors, are harmful. Recently there has been an attack planned to be performed against Bitcoin, named SegWit2x (not to be confused with SegWit). Several large companies using Bitcoin, and the majority of miners, have tried to hijack the development of Bitcoin, to give it to their own corporate-backed developers [15]. The whole Bitcoin community fought together to prevent this from happening, and in the end, they emerged victorious – the attack was canceled a few weeks before its supposed date [16]. This is similar to what happens in nature, when the whole biotope reacts to and defends itself from a foreign invader, especially if it threatens to destroy the whole habitat. This is similar to a human organism reacting to and defending itself from a virus.

There are several scenarios of how cryptocurrencies might evolve in the future. One possible way is for one or several of the largest cryptocurrencies to survive, while all others become obsolete. This is akin to situations in nature, where one or several species become dominant and extinguish other competing species. This can happen even without specifically trying to eradicate another species, an example of which is how Homo Sapiens wiped out Neanderthals by spreading diseases which infected the Neanderthals and sped up their annihilation[98].

Blockchain technology is at an evolutionary juncture. Will the future be dominated by permissioned or permission-less blockchain technology, or could the two coexist? Darwinian history has shown that, competing and analogous species tend to coexist for extended periods of time, until there is a divergence, creating separate species, sometimes ones that are vastly different or sometimes one obliterating the other[99].

The future of blockchain may be a social experiment for the betterment of humanity[100]. These solutions could be either benevolent, or malevolent, or both. As the world becomes more polarized and populism ascends[101], nation states and countries might choose individual interests and self-preservation.

Private and consensus blockchains[102], might be given exclusive legitimacy. These blockchains' efficiency benefits could be exploited but their permissioned qualities, that are inherently centralized and hierarchical, where monopolistic and oligopolistic tendencies thrive, will be promoted. Russia might issue its own state cryptocurrency[103]. China, in theory, has heavily regulated its domestic cryptocurrency space, but in practice, it still wants to utilize the benefits of the technology, albeit within the sphere of China's control and centralized infrastructure.

Nation states and countries if they provide the infrastructure that solves the "last mile issue", could permit blockchain technology to evolve, but it would be in a permissioned ecosystem, that will be highly censored and nationalistic.

Another possibility is for thousands of cryptocurrencies to continue to exist, in an interconnected and inter-operable way (cryptocurrencies are already very easily inter-operable), for example using some sort of meta-protocol to easily move between cryptocurrencies. Such technology already exists and is called Atomic Swaps (although for it to be able to be used, both cryptocurrencies must support the Lightning Network, so as a prerequisite for that they both need SegWit or another type of transaction malleability fix integrated). This is similar to how in nature different species develop equilibrium and symbiotic inter-species relationships, helping each other to find food, shelter, or otherwise improving each other's odds of survival[104].

What is clear, regardless of how the cryptocurrency and blockchain landscape evolves, blockchain technology will be used more and more widely in the future, as it offers huge benefits for companies, such as cost reduction, increased traceability, disintermediation, censorship resistance, data immutability, and other[105].

New cryptocurrencies will continue being created and will keep trying to improve on various aspects of cryptocurrencies and Blockchain technology. However, there might soon come a time where new methods of such software evolving will be possible. One of the most likely cases of where/how it might happen is ransomware. Ransomware is a computer software which locks (encrypts) files on a user's computer without their consent, and then requests a ransom to be paid in cryptocurrency to unlock the files. Such software also tries to spread itself to other computers using various methods, such as emailing itself to all contacts in the original user's contact book, trying to look for network vulnerabilities to be able to spread to other computers connected to the same network etc.[106] While at the moment such software is created by some particular developer or group of developers, and spreads without making any random changes in itself, it might be possible to develop ransomware which would make random changes in its code before spreading, therefore emulating biological evolution.

Another method would be to create modular ransomware software which would function completely autonomously, and which would use the money collected from ransoms to hire programmers to improve it, as well as purchase hosting, VPN access, or any other services which might improve its chance to collect more ransoms. If it was modular, any improvement made by a particular programmer could be made in such a way that the programmer who codes the particular change would receive some part of the ransom money as well, thus incentivizing programmers to work on such software. While this method would be a little bit different from the biological evolution than the aforementioned method of random changes, it would still be closer to biological evolution than the current traditional methods of software development.

If we ignore the current limitations of blockchain technology, the future might look even more promising than described above. Security of the Internet-of-Things is an issue. In the world of the smart city, with many IoT devices transmitting information, security will be of utmost importance. Technology has been evolving rapidly, but security has lagged[107]. If IoT devices malfunction or are sabotaged – the results can be fatal. Self-flying airplanes crashing, mistakes during automated surgery, lift bridges opening at the wrong time, etc. It is predicted that the blockchain can resolve IoT's security issues. As one potential solution, IoT devices could be embedded with Plantoids – a Blockchain-Based Artificial Life. Plantoids are autonomous entities which are completely independent and self-sufficient. An ecosystem designed for spontaneous Darwinian-like evolution. The non-visible part of a Plantoid is a DAO – a Distributed Autonomous Organization with a set of smart contracts that manage the Plantoid's life cycle and reproduction[108].

Environment has a huge impact in Darwinian-like evolution. Some male insects elicit dominance in their environment and assure the propagation of their genes. For example, bees and fruit flies influence the behavior and physiology of their female mates, when they inject semen into them[109]. In the case of the female fruit fly, after she is impregnated, her rate of egg laying increases, her receptivity to mating with other fruit fly's decreases, and her life span shortens. She also stores the male fruit fly's sperm, thus guaranteeing future continuance of his genes. Darwin natural selection - survival of the fittest is at play in these insects' mating ritual, ultimately controlling the fertility of unwanted insects[110].

Plantoid entities in IoT devices are in many ways like insects; the dominant and most effective and efficient iterations will be the preferred choices to be embedded (impregnated) into IoT devices. Thus, these Plantoids, like those lucky bees and fruit flies, will propagate. Lesser Plantoids will be discarded, become extinct. IoT devices will need to navigate very hostile and fluid environments. Plantoid type smart contracts embedded in these devices would need to recalibrate and recreate themselves on the fly. A smart city of the future will not be smart, if its IoT devices continuously collide with each other, or even worse, crash into you. It remains to be seen which cryptocurrencies will fuel these smart contracts. But in Darwinian-like evolution, the one that facilitates the adaption of this technology wins. A cryptocurrency that is used in billions of IoT devices wields enormous influence.

Evolution of cryptocurrencies and Blockchain technology has a lot of parallels with the natural world, and in many situations behaves and responds in patterns reminiscent to those seen in nature. As Blockchain technology is based on programming code and can therefore incorporate other innovations made in information technologies such as artificial intelligence, in the future blockchain technology will most likely follow the laws of natural selection even more closely than it does now and can perhaps even be a part of what we would call a "self-aware" or at least "fully-autonomous" artificial intelligence. We can see digital currencies to be the only form in which a computer can charge humans for their work. We would like to extend this work further to develop a holistic theory of evolution for crypto currencies keeping in mind Adam Smith's invisible hand and build a framework for blockchain to analyze, monitor and enhance the future evolutionary changes in this space.

~~~~~

Ethereum Mining

A lot of people are curious about how Ethereum is mined. In this chapter, you will learn a simple way to mine Ethereum, Ethereum classic and all those cryptocurrencies which can be mined using Graphical Processing Unit (GPU).

The following is a step-by-step procedure.

1. To start with, you have to create your 'wallet' through the website MyEtherWallet. It is as simple as choosing and entering a password and clicking on a button.

Figure 1.

2. Next, save the Keystroke file on your hard disk.

Figure 2.

3. Copy and paste your Private Key onto a secure location so that you don't forget it. If you lose this key, you will be unable to access your wallet and any funds available in it will go to waste.

Figure 3.

4. Now, open your wallet using the Keystroke / JSON File option or Private Key option.

Figure 4.

5. After clicking Unlock button, scroll down and you will be able to see that your wallet currently contains no funds.

Figure 5.

6. Next, search for Clay More mines on Google and download it.

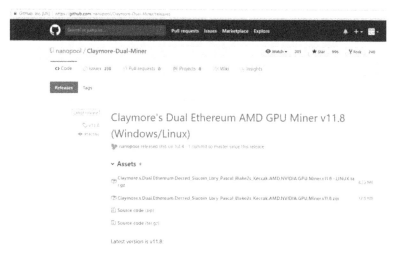

Figure 6.

7. Go to the website Nano Pool and click on the Quick Start on 'Ethereum'

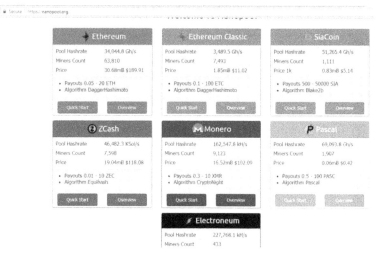

Figure 7.

8. Click on 'Generate your config' button.

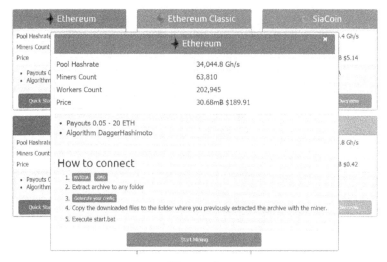

Figure 8.

9. In the popup window, choose OS and GPU options as per your requirement. Select Asia as the Main server and Ethereum as First Algorithm.

Figure 9.

10. After downloading the 'Config' file, copy it on the Clay More folder and run Start File.

Figure 10.

11. Go back to Nano Pool and in the address bar, enter your wallet address.

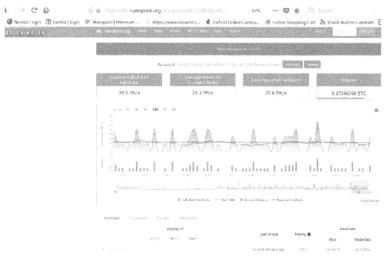

Figure 11.

12. Congratulations! You are mining.

In order to mine another coin, choose that specification from the Nano Pool and create a Config file. If you wish to create a 'mining farm' with lots of machines, then first visit the mining section of the CryptoCompare website in order to ascertain whether or not this endeavor will be profitable for you at all. Normally, if your electricity cost is more than 6 PKR/unit, you will not gain substantial benefit from mining. In Pakistan, a unit costs up to 15 PKR.

Figure 12.

Figure 13.

You can see a test mining farm in the following pictures. This is located in the USA, where electricity is cheaper. With

12 GPU cards (about 200 MHZ), about 0.4 to 0.5 Ethereum can be mined every month, costing you around 700,000 PKR.

Figure 14.

Figure 15.

Figure 16.

~~~~~

Some Questions for Esteemed Religious Scholars

As blockchain and cryptocurrency is quite the word these days, and a significant number of people are joining the bandwagon, we wish to put forward the following few questions before you so that you may guide us on these points. We will include your answers accurately and faithfully in the next edition.

What do esteemed Islamic jurists and scholars say about the following:

1. What is the Islamic definition of 'money'? From the Islamic point of view, what is it that we can identify as 'money'?

2. What is the difference between 'money' and 'currency'?

3. Does the definition of 'money' appear in the Holy Quran and Ahadith or has this been derived from tradition or scholarly opinion?

4. Is blockchain, a public account / facility for financial transactions, in itself permissible or non-permissible?

5. Will you declare digital currency, created via the complex mathematics of cryptography, non-permissible?

6. Bitcoin and other cryptocurrencies like it, such as Ethereum, Litecoin and Ripple, all originated with the help of blockchain and cryptography and are fast gaining popularity among the public. Do these, in themselves, contain some culpability from the Islamic point of view?

7. Some people also utilize cryptocurrency for illegal tasks, for example in the trade of drugs or payment of crime. In such cases, will this specific use of cryptocurrency be non-permissible or will the cryptocurrency itself be non-permissible?

8. If, keeping the public's welfare and ignorance in mind, you declare cryptocurrency to be non-permissible from

the perspective of potential damage, would you clarify that this is being said in the interest of the public, and not that cryptocurrency on its own merit is non-permissible?

9. No doubt, the 21st century is characterized by inventions and new, uncharted technology. Specific examples of many of these - such as WhatsApp, Facebook, Instagram, internet, online banking, etc. - are not to be found mentioned in the Quran, Sunnah and Islamic tradition. In these circumstances, is it permissible to gain education and knowledge about these new technologies in order to better understand them and become aware of whether or not they are aligned to the spirit of Islam?

10. In light of the corruption, pillage and disrepute of governments, people are fast losing trust in central institutions and are searching for alternate systems. Cryptocurrency and blockchain offer such a system. Must we continue to tolerate oppression or could we incline towards another system in order to improve our lives?

Please do give counsel; it will benefit many. May Allah reward you.

~~~~~

Use Cases

Use Case - Pakistan General Elections on Blockchain

The history of elections and the charges of corruption, voters' fraud, ghost votes, interferences by deep state and violence go hand in hand. There is (almost) no country in the world spared from suspicions or accusations of such incidents in elections. Whether it is Russia's meddling[111] in the US elections or the alleged role of Cambridge Analytica[112] to sway voters one way or other, 92 people getting killed[113] in Kenya's election or 31 in Honduras[114], 80 candidates losing their lives in Mexico[115] or 11 in Assam, India[116], 74 in Pakistan's[117] last elections[118] or 174 in recent elections - election fraud and rigging[119] would find its roots in all the incidents.

Can blockchain solve all or at least some of these issues — counterfeit votes, rigging, changes in records after the polls, physical suppression of voters at polling booths, fifty shades of electoral fraud and violence during elections? How about cost saving for this multi-billion dollar global industry?

Blockchain is being used worldwide from health care to refugee registration, from supply chain management to a sexual harassment complaint registry, from property records to humanitarian assistance, and from transferring remittances to auctioning art and antiques. It can also be used to change the way elections are being conducted throughout the world, for example by increasing voters' participation, enhancing security, efficiency, and transparency of ballots, reducing election violence, eliminating electoral fraud and corruption, and improving reliability, safety, affordability, and access to the system.

Pia Mancini has brilliantly articulated in her Ted talk[120], "We are 21st-century citizens, dealing with 19th-century institutions, that are formed on the basis of 15th-century information technology" and explored various ideas about what we can and should do to upgrade the system. DemocracyOS[121] is what came out of her work and is worth reading.

Running Pakistan's elections on blockchain is as easy as the following. Election Commission of Pakistan (ECP) would issue a unit of specialized tokens to all eligible voters after due verification and enrollment. All candidates will have their own wallet. Verified voters will be able to transfer the tokens back to their chosen candidates' addresses with transparency, security, and reliability of a public ledger while keeping their identities anonymous. The voting token cannot be used before the voting date and time and will automatically "burn" by a smart contract when the time ends. At the end of the day, the candidate with maximum number of tokens would win.

The concerned parties can easily observe and verify the results on public ledger without the need for lengthy legal procedures that cause instability with claims of wrongdoing. The verification process will rely on the underlying blockchain technology without central control to make it as transparent and unbiased as it can get. Anyone can verify the results and identify inconsistencies. This eliminates the possibility of electoral fraud, manipulation of results, and the miscalculation and misrepresentation of tallies.

To keep the voters anonymous, the token issuing authority (say ECP or NADRA) would verify the voters through their CNIC/NICOP/Passports and issue them a private unique ID. Voters can then use that ID to vote on a public blockchain, so while anyone can confirm the real voter by his/her unique ID, no one can find out who the voter is. The issuing authority can also use a cryptography-based masking algorithm, zero-knowledge proof, ring transaction, or a fancy encryption technique to generate the IDs which they cannot decode by themselves either (for example by trying to reverse engineer and map the actual voters with submitted votes).

There still remain a few challenges though, for example verifying whether the citizen has the right to vote in a particular jurisdiction in the first place. A citizen's eligibility to vote needs a central authority to confirm, and then the mechanism to make sure that the person who just got confirmed will be the same person at the time of voting is another nightmare.

These technical challenges can easily be overcome with the appropriate technical and intellectual capital, innovation and cryptography methods available today. Given the advantages of blockchain technology, we should pilot it in bi-elections and come up with a national plan to switch to blockchain-based voting in the near future.

Think about the advantages such a system has to offer. It will increase transparency to start with. When you vote in the current system, you have no idea what happened to your vote - was it counted at all, was it counted right? There exists no way to go back and confirm that. With blockchain, anyone can check their vote, and how it got counted, after the polls on a public ledger. It will eliminate rigging altogether as it would be impossible to cheat the cryptographic-governance of the blockchain ledger. It will be fast, as all counting and tally can happen in real-time. It will save billions of rupees, as there will be no need for polling stations, security staff, presiding officers, no need to transport millions of people to polling stations, no traffic jams, no *biryani* and no terrorism threats for the masses. Moreover, it can increase voters' turn-out by allowing almost everyone to vote from the comfort of their homes, offices or even outside the country. People inside prisons or living overseas can vote too.

Furthermore, all technical details and blockchain complexities can be automated and hidden under a user-friendly GUI (application layer) where the user has to select the image of the party symbol or picture of his/her favorite candidate and press a button to transfer the token from his wallet to the chosen candidate's address. It will also increase voters' participation through mobile phones, sparing them the commute to distant polling stations and the risk of facing thuggish maneuvers to influence their choice.

Any claims raised by the opposition on validity, counting or transparency of votes can instantly be checked and confirmed by any party on public blockchain ledger in no time. ECP can publish the whole register the very next day in the media so everyone can check if his or her vote was counted right through their unique IDs. It will save legal costs, delays in forming the government and will reduce the frustration and anxiety of indecision that usually generates after-shocks of violent national unrest.

There are several examples of blockchain based voting systems worldwide, like VoteWatcher[122], VoteUnits[123], Democracy Earth[124], MIT TR35 winner Jorge Garcia's VotoSocial[125], Follow My Vote[126], Agora[127]—the company behind Sierra Leone claimed and then debunked[128] blockchain voting and even real-time blockchain based voting for national issues where the voter has the flexibility to cast a vote or withdraw the support for a candidate or proposal even after the elections, a concept called Liquid Democracy[129] through United Vote[130]. There is also a patent[131] of how to count and secure votes on the blockchain.

Free and Fair[132] offers an open-source voting technology, Voatz[133] has recently made a debut[134] to provide voting facility to on-duty veterans outside the country and Votem[135] is the first mobile-based global voting solution. However, there are always cyber threats and drawbacks of such systems, like India's Adhaar information[136] found to be available online to purchase, and Pakistan's NADRA data being sold publicly on Facebook[137].

One can learn how to develop such systems online. There is a course by Zastrin to help build a voting application on Ethereum for free[138], a live demo of voting dApp,[139] and an example of a smart contract in Solidity[140] for a voting application.

Following is the basic voting smart contract (a modified version of *Remix* example) to start with.

pragma solidity ^0.4.0;

contract PakistanElections {

```
struct Voter {
uint weight;
bool voted;
uint8 vote;
address delegate;
}
struct Candidate {
uint voteCount;
}
address ecp;
mapping(address => Voter) voters;
Candidate[] candidates;
/// Create a new PakistanElections with $(_numCandidates
) different candidate.
function PakistanElections(uint8 _numCandidates) public {
ecp = msg.sender;
voters[ecp].weight = 1;
candidates.length = _numCandidates;
}
/// Give $(toVoter) the right to vote on this
PakistanElections.
/// May only be called by $(ecp).
function giveRightToVote(address toVoter) public {
if (msg.sender != ecp || voters[toVoter].voted) return;
voters[toVoter].weight = 1;
}
/// Delegate your vote to the voter $(to).
function delegate(address to) public {
Voter storage sender = voters[msg.sender]; // assigns
reference
```

```
if (sender.voted) return;

while    (voters[to].delegate   !=    address(0)    &&
voters[to].delegate != msg.sender)

to = voters[to].delegate;

if (to == msg.sender) return;

sender.voted = true;

sender.delegate = to;

Voter storage delegateTo = voters[to];

if (delegateTo.voted)

candidates[delegateTo.vote].voteCount += sender.weight;

else

delegateTo.weight += sender.weight;

}

/// Give a single vote to candidate $(toCandidate).

function vote(uint8 toCandidate) public {

Voter storage sender = voters[msg.sender];

if (sender.voted || toCandidate >= candidates.length)
return;

sender.voted = true;

sender.vote = toCandidate;

candidates[toCandidate].voteCount += sender.weight;

}

function winningCandidate() public constant returns (uint8
_winningCandidate) {

uint256 winningVoteCount = 0;

for (uint8 prop = 0; prop < candidates.length; candi++)

if (candidates[candi].voteCount > winningVoteCount) {

winningVoteCount = candidates[candi].voteCount; }

}

}
```

Use Case – SexBlock
(Global Registry for Sexual Harassment on Blockchain)

The United States alone encounters more than 10,000[141] cases of sexual harassment at the workplace each year on average. The economic cost of these incidents is estimated to be over $1 billion in US[1] and $4 billion[142] worldwide and yet there is no scalable global solution available to record the details of events and the names of the prime accused. SexBlock is a blockchain based open public registry to record, monitor and maintain the details of convicted sexual harassers. Call it a Yelp for #MeToo incidents.

DLT's inherent advantage of immutability will make it impossible to alter or remove the data once it is recorded, thus making it a priceless resource to make this world a safer place. It will be scalable, cost effective (running on public permission-less blockchain), and can help raise funds for sexual assault victims through its own native currency – M2C (MeTooCoin).

Sexual harassment happens on a daily basis all over the world and posits the need of a common registry without centralized interference to record such incidents. The complete process, from filing a complaint to uploading evidence, legal advice and case filings can be done via smart contract and automation[143]. It can also become a precedent for other future cases.

Recalling our list of questions in Chapter Three, this use case satisfies all of the questions to be a promising application for blockchain.

It is an ongoing and repetitive process. Sexual harassment cases usually have long processes that run for months if not years. There are many parties involved: the accuser, the accused, the legal system, lawyers, media and employers along with the families and colleagues from each side. The blockchain-based solution will help put everything together in one place and would serve to be a handy reference in future.

There are many stakeholders in this process - from the main accused and accuser to legal systems, local government agencies like the employment bureau, labor commissioner office, media and correction institutes. Additionally, there is always a public interest and political backing on these cases as well.

There are diverse data silos in this use case that can be solved by blockchain. There is data and evidence from the accuser, there is counter data from the employer or the accused, there are legal and financial proceedings, there are settlement claims and there is data from open social networks and media about the case.

To retain one's honor is of great value. In the majority of cases, the accused do not want to come out openly in the interests of their honor and privacy. Blockchain will give them (and witnesses) the anonymity they need and still be able to register and process the case. The real value that lies in the process is of the safeguarding of dignity and economic losses for all parties.

People and bosses move from one workplace to another, one city to another and one country to another, only to find the next prey and repeat the hostilities again. The global scalable and immutable registry will restrict them to repeat the same process again. It will make it difficult for bad guys to hide in plain sight.

Let's examine the user case with the proposed layers system from Chapter Three.

Protocol Layer:

It will be a public blockchain with its own native currency MeTooCoin (M2C) as value tokens to incentivize participation from all stakeholders. The participant nodes can "verify" the state of affairs via consensus protocol. The validators and reporters can confirm the transaction and trigger the ending set of commands such as arriving at settlements or issuing press releases or evidence to media outlets, as programmed by smart contracts.

It will use Ethereum platform. Its current speed of 15 transactions per second is good enough for this application and there is a large community and developers at GitHub to support and extend it frequently. There is also a growing supply for Ethereum smart contract programmers in Solidity and Viper.

Network Layer:

For network layer, we should consider the following technical properties for this application:

1. **Immutability:** We should have recourse to correct the errors before confirming it permanently

2. **Security:** We should ensure that the network remains secure from malicious users and accidental mistakes

3. **Confidentiality:** As anyone can see the entire contents, we need to be aware of geographical laws and limitations as we are dealing with the very sensitive issue of sexual harassment

4. **Quality of Data:** Smart contracts need a secure bridge with external data. We need to consider how to add interoperability with other platforms and non-distributed apps (nDApps).

5. **Language:** Which language is the smart contract designed in? How would its evolution change the interaction and design of our app?

6. **Clients:** Which client to use and work with – Geth? Parity, Claymore? Which one is more secure, easily accessible and cost effective?

7. **Frameworks:** Which framework is the smart contract using? Meteor, Maven, Truffle, Embark, Zeppelin? What are the security, accessibility and cost trade-offs?

8. **Best Practices:** Are we following the best practices of the business domain?

9. **Storage:** Are we storing all the data on blockchain itself or can we use some decentralized storage like Swarm or IPFS? Can we only store hashes on blockchain and everything else on a decentralized storage system?

10. **Costs:** What are the costs associated with the smart contract and what it would take to keep it running? Here we can use the native currency to pay for the services to Ethereum platform.

Application Layer:

The application is going to be used by many stakeholders from prime accused to accuser, and from legal systems to employer, media and the public. The current economic cost of sexual harassment is $699 million for settlement payments, $350 million for legal fee, and $125,000 per case for loss of work [3]. The proposed app will give an economical, reliable and fast way to accomplish the complete processing.

Currently, the whole process takes anywhere from a few months to a few years from lodging the complaint to the relevant authorities to producing witnesses in court, and from legal filing to financial payments and settlements. Blockchain can replace the whole paper-based system with an immutable global scalable DLT register. This autonomy will increase traceability, efficiency, productivity, transparency, provenance, trust and loyalty throughout the supply chain – processes, technology and people.

SexBlock through smart contract is a digital protocol to enforce performance, and verify and negotiate the contract among two or more parties. It is an algorithmic way to record and process sexual harassment claims. It is an attempt to interpret Ricardian contracts to algorithmic rules to process it via automation.

We can see a backlash from the legal system and lawyers in particular for using such a technology as they will lose a major chunk of legal fees and the processing time they need to pressurize the counter party to submit to their wish. Perhaps, blockchain will give us a more balanced society, free from inherent biases of the centralized systems we have today.

This use case takes a holistic view and seeks to explore blockchain to solve the sexual harassment problem across the world. It will help us define a framework and identify the links, resources, formats, and types of data to make a public ledger of sexual harassment where researchers can perform statistical analysis and deploy a nation-wide system to observe and prevent this phenomena using permission-less blockchain.

SexBlock research can serve many objectives, such as building a minimal viable product to test the viability and technical limits of this idea. Further, it can explore how we can optimize it at later stage, identify how timely is the idea with market needs and its worthiness for impact, figure out what strengths - human capital, finances, government and international players' needs and requirements - would be needed to make it happen, identify dataset formatting, cleaning, modeling and ownership, identify and record the relationship between dataset and the owner organization and the pathways to disseminate that knowledge, store and format the datasets in a common shareable format over blockchain, design and deploy a nation-wide census data platform for government, and last but not least, define a framework to combine multiple data sources over blockchain for collective modelling for social impact.

~~~~~

Use Case – Pakistan National Census on Blockchain

Conducting national census on a permissionless blockchain is a robust, scalable, transparent, immutable and temper-proof solution to conduct the national census for a country. It solves the problem of missing persons (US Congress, 2012)[144] in census using blockchain by utilizing multiple and diverse community-level datasets to verify the individual's living condition and address (Alan & MacDonald 2005)[145].

Population census is a mandatory requirement by the UN for almost all countries (Hinckley, 2012)[146] and serves to provide a basis for governments' financial, economic, health and education policies for its populace (Joe, Clairece & Booher 2011)[147]. Census plays a very important role in mapping a country's growth and financial trajectories and it is the single most valuable and shared resource among government departments and apparatuses. It is generally public, non-classified, and has multiple stakeholders (Reynolds & John 2000)[148]. Immutability of records is required and appreciated (William 2011)[149], thus making it an ideal candidate for the permissionless blockchain solution.

There are a few drawbacks with the current system by design – data update of each individual is a laborious and repeatable process and there is a dire need to protect the rights of minorities and marginalized communities against corrupt government and selfish potentates (US Congress 2012, Swaroop 2018)[150]. Statistical ethnic-cleansing and misrepresentation of minorities has been witnessed in Nigeria's census (Abraham, 1999)[151]. As much as 1.5 million people from the city of Karachi have been reported missing from the recent Pakistan's census of 2017 (Karim, 2017[152], Israr 2017)[153], and the United States missed 15 million people from minorities in its 2010 census (CBS, 2012)[154]. The US will be using internet-based survey and verification for 2020 census to solve part of this problem (Census, 2016)[155].

Moreover, transparency, quality and accuracy of data and safeguarding personally identifiable information (PII) are few other challenges for the current system (Margo 2015)[156]. Transforming and conducting the census on blockchain has the inherent advantages of security, transparency and immutability with the added element of societal value to record, monitor, forecast and extrapolate the country's demographic dynamics and socio-economic activities. It can also yield socio-economic benefits.

One can also incentivize the participation by giving control of data back to its user, i.e. self-sovereign identity. The user will be able to own the rights of their data and claim government subsidies and social security against it (Maureen2015)[157]. Census has been used for various purposes from GIS mapping to ecological surveys (William 2006)[158], it can also be monetized for marketing and research – anyone who uses the data has to pay (in native currency of the system, say Centura) to that citizen – from behavioral modelling to offering targeted ads.

This use case sits at the cross-roads of computer science, surveying, government internal affairs, blockchain, hyper-ledger, human development index and statistics, allowing cross-pollination of ideas, technology and governing framework. We expect to research and define a solution for missing persons in Census through a framework for citizens-as-a-service using plug-n-play chaincode containers.

Blockchain is a peer-to-peer decentralized distributed ledger that permanently records and guarantees an immutable, unalterable trustworthy transaction (of money or any valuable asset) in a trust-less environment chronologically through consensus protocol secured by cryptography with economically incentivized participation (Usmani, 2018)[159]. It is an immutable, open, secure and transparent shared ledger that anyone can voluntarily join and leave at will. It has two broad types: Public (with open participation, incentivized and punished by consensus protocol) and Private (with consortium or private businesses' vetted membership and enforcement of laws and regulations in place.) (George, 2018)[160]. Compared to centralized structures, blockchain saves time, removes cost, reduces risk and increases trust. Blockchain technology offers many benefits and advantages over traditional centuries' old centralized systems. The advantages range from security to efficiency and from immutability to non-alterability (Daniel, 2017)[161]

Under the United Nation's convention on the Rights of the Child, article 8, the right to identity is one of the fundamental human rights to peruse ones' social, cultural, economic and political well-being (OHCHR, 1989)[162]. Identity-as-a-Service seems like a natural application of such a system where citizens do not have to rely on their governments and have to go through a plethora of ID verifications while doing international travelling, businesses or transactions. One of the key advantages is to be able to use "One ID" for everything to be able to confirm you are you. It is also easy to maintain, secure, validate and justify with inherent advantages of speed, updates, immutability and control.

Like any new and emerging technology, it is hard to extrapolate and forecast the future implications and drawbacks of switching to an entirely new system that has not been battle-tested (Don, 2016)[163]. One of the issues with using blockchain for identification management is its public availability and lack of privacy. For example, anyone can access and see the contents of a block in a blockchain. Without proper rules and steps to reveal what kind of information one wants to release in what particular situation, it would be hard to stop a malicious user to gain access of one's identity details that he/she can later use to impersonate (Paul, 2018)[164]. Another problem might come due to speed of verification process, for example, someone is crossing an international border and verification over the blockchain would take 15 minutes per individual, in that case the throughput of the immigration at borders would be very slow, thus restricting the inflow of visitors and choking the entire airport operations.

We would like to explore the government sector with the focus area of the census department. As mentioned earlier, census is mandatory to take place by the UN every ten years in almost all countries. Population census provides the basis for governments' financial, economic, health and education policies for its populace and this is how the current state of affairs and forecasting for the country's well-being is calculated on granular levels (William, 2011)[165]. Census plays a very important role in mapping a country's growth and financial trajectory and it is the single most valuable and shared resource that is used among numerous departments and apparatuses of the government. It is, in almost all cases, non-classified and generally available to download from public websites, thus making it an ideal candidate for the blockchain solution (Reynolds & John 2000)[166].

Our aim in this use case is to understand and transfer the inner workings of the census project to a practical blockchain. We aim to solve the missing persons problem, which is one of the hardest to overcome all over the world. We also aim to explore the benefits it would yield for the country and its people, and seek to overcome the current problems and bureaucratic hurdles in the current census system by using blockchain technology.

There are a few traits that exist in the census project. The immutability of records, for example, is required and appreciated. Data update of each individual is a tiresome and repetitive process, and there is the element of societal value inherent in such a system. Moreover, there are multiple parties involved in this system and there is need for open and transparent processing to protect the rights of minorities and marginalized communities against corrupt government and selfish potentates.

There could be multiple ways to support such a system with supplied value. First, it has an immense social value to record, monitor, forecast and extrapolate a country's inner structure and dynamics based on its population behaviour. This alone can yield benefits for health, education and well-being of its people. We can also incentivize participation by giving control of data back to its user. Users will be able to own the rights of their data and claim government's subsidies and social security against it. It can also be monetized for marketing and research; anyone who uses the data has to pay (in native currency of the system, say Centura) to that citizen – from behavioral modelling to offering targeted ads. DevPost has developed a blockchain based census system for Catalonia's referendum (Ivan, 2017)[167]. NovaTeqni has introduced a blockchain based device to capture census data during user interviews (NovaTeqni, 2017)[168]. It provides the transparency, security and scalability of blockchain to solve regular problems of data manipulation, such as losses and delays at data recording level during population interviews.

The intended audience for this work is the government's statistical department responsible for conducting census, companies involved in government work or demographics research, and the general population at large.

In fact, the total addressable market for census on blockchain is the current population of the country. Every single individual in the country is going to benefit with such a system. We can also extend this market by incorporating all the companies using data to drive network and advertisement traffic in and out of the country and to include foreign visitors and expats. Having the information of visiting expats on public blockchain would increase the monetization potential of such a system many folds. The worldwide data market value is to the tune of 1 trillion dollars annually (World Economic Forum, 2017)[169].

This application is aimed for countries with large Muslim populations. Muslim countries generally have three set of laws that are not mutually exclusive and can differ in interpretation, context and consequences. Most counties have adopted the Sharia law following the Hanafi, Shafi, Hanbali, Maliki or Shia' school of thought - the uncodified law based on Islamic principles (Quran and Hadith) (Frank, 2000)[170]. The second set of laws comes from the executive orders - the orders passed by the chief executive officer of the country The third set of laws comes from penal code used by the country – British penal code for most of South Asia for example (Hooker, 1978)[171]. The evolving nature of these laws under no precedents makes it a fertile ground for innovation and to launch blockchain solutions.

The majority of the laws and regulations are principle based, following the Islamic orthodox interpretations of world affairs. If something is permissible in Islam, it will be allowed by the law regardless of what it meant for the world, humanitarian organizations, local businesses or international law. If something is not permissible under Islam, like alcoholic beverages, pork or interest on savings, it will not be allowed in the country regardless of its perceived benefits to society at large (Frank, 2000)[172].

Local regulations for this use case focus on the outcomes without getting into the technical details and underlying legal compliances. Once the system is through the agreed-upon principles according to Shaira Laws, it will be smooth sailing for the rest of the procedures and regulations of the country. The current legal system of Islamic countries in general, focuses more on outcome rather than the means to get there.

The blockchain solution on hyper-ledger chaincode also takes care of all the stakeholders from government, to political parties, ethnic minorities, public departments and population at large. It can be done through regulatory sandbox and this would be the first ever Sharia-compliant regulatory sandbox for blockchain in the world. Since it is based on DLT (Distributed Ledger Technology), it fosters trust among all stakeholders and increases transparency and fairness while promoting competition. Due to immutability nature of DLT records on the public ledger of census, everyone can see, monitor, examine and flag any conflict-of-interest and this will make it a very competitive data marketplace where data is owned by citizens themselves.

The use case will provide an equal playing field for all the parties to build upon DApps on this massive census platform and will get it out of the government's hands.

Census is a government affair since the beginning with little access to anyone else for innovation. This use case aims to define and create a new market from scratch. There are a few players in the market who are somewhat trying to develop similar tools, but they are all focusing on telecom or financial data. Our application aims to get all publicly available datasets from census to provide a holistic picture of customers' life events. This is the gap we like to address to create a unique market proposition for our investors, customers and partners.

Census usually relies on physically canvassing the neighborhood for on-site counting, and some of the state-run programs database for address verification like health, food or other social help programs. The "missing persons" remain invisible due to their hard-to-count-living-circumstances like unregistered buildings, non-compliant house extensions, unusual living conditions (basement, parking garages, several families sharing the same residence due to housing cost, homeless shelters, under the tree or on-the-wheels). Ethnic and racial minorities and illegal immigrants disproportionately and intentionally live under-the-radar to escape legal consequences. Blockchain can solve this problem by combining related databases from the community, like local church and shelter donations, food programs, second language and adult learning centers, local parcel delivery and health visitors' database, transportation like local busses and ride-sharing services, community or state-run nutrition services, temporary assistance programs and legal help datasets. The immutability and privacy of blockchain can serve the undocumented population of our societies through various means and get the confirmation from community run consensus protocol.

To respond to a census questionnaire is not mandatory and cannot be forced by law. Several countries are working to add citizenship status in census that will further decrease the response rate. Blockchain based solution is much needed to research and help in this area by combining non-state databases to record, verify and secure the missing population from national census all over the world.

This use case takes a holistic view on the aforementioned perspectives. The lack of transparency, immutability of records and aggregation of socio-economic indicators across the nation poses a daunting task to accomplish using standard technologies. This application sets to explore blockchain and hyper-ledger fabric to solve the national census task for countries, specifically solving the missing person problem. It will help us define the framework and identify the links, resources, formats, and types of data for the national census where researchers can perform statistical analysis and deploy a nation-wide system to observe the national socio-economic health using permissionless blockchain.

This use case has the following research objectives:

- To identify and define *Proof-of-Curiosity* – how timely is the idea vis-à-vis market needs and our available strengths to take it forward – human capital, finances, government and international players' needs and requirements – and the worthiness of the idea for impact and generalization, support of bi-products and peripheral innovation.

- To identify and define *Proof-of-Due-Diligence for Missing Person* – how we can build a proof-of-concept or MVP to test the viability and technical limits of this idea? What are the lessons learned during the process and how we can optimize it?

- To identify and define *Proof-of-Ownership* – Who will take the plunge, who will invest time and resources, where will the funding come from? Who will be the beta customers, who will be the partners and data providers? How would the project incentivize and give the due share to all the people involved in this from beginning.

- To identify the dataset formatting, cleaning, modeling and ownership

- To identify and record the relationship between dataset and the owner organization and the pathways to disseminate that knowledge

- To store and format the datasets in a common shareable format over blockchain

- To design and implement chaincode containers over hyper-ledger for business logic

- To design and deploy a nation-wide census data platform for government and corporates

- To define a framework to combine multiple data sources over blockchain for collective modelling for the social impact

We will be collecting the data from Pakistan's statistics department as our primary source. We are targeting to get the data of 5 million citizens from five major cities for this use case – Karachi, Lahore, Islamabad, Peshawar and Quetta (to get the unbiased representative sample of the whole country). The data will be from the recent census of 2017.

We are expecting 5 million rows of data with 53 categories each (5000 x 53 = 265,000 dimensions). It will help us understand the inner workings of the census data and the inherent biases the data has to start with. Once data collection is done, we will analyse and devise a blockchain-as-a-platform based architecture to define it with proper data dictionaries and matrices to be able to perform both quantitative and qualitative analyses. We will use data science, predictive analytics and deep learning toolsets like SciKit, TensorFlow, Random Forest to analyse the quantitative data and visualization toolsets like Tableau, QLikView and Pentaho for visual story telling of the system.

~~~~~

Use Case – Supply Chain Management

The aim of supply chain is to provide transparency while keeping track of quantity and quality of goods it ships from starting point to the end delivery point. However, it is too complex, fragmented, costly and geographically divided with various laws and regulations. These challenges make it inaccurate, inefficient and slow to begin with. Most of supply chain happens in the ocean and thus exposes the goods to extreme temperatures and prolonged periods of travel, heavy paperwork, and multiple costs at each point of the journey. Illicit activities occur due to loopholes in international laws and paperwork at each point in the chain with no or very minimal visibility.

To find out if the supply chain will be a good problem to solve through blockchain, we will revisit the questionnaire discussed in chapter 3.

In almost all cases of product development, the process can be performed via automation. For example, if you are making undergarments, the whole supply chain from clothing to stiches and from ribbons to wires can be placed on blockchain for ordering, payment, transparency, monitoring, and fiduciary purposes.

Supply chains usually have long-running transactions or processes that run repeatedly or continuously in some cases. Going back to our example of undergarments, we need to order clothing and ribbons for the manufacturing facility and once the product is designed and stitched it will go to the shipping department. This cycle is repeated every time.

There are multiple stakeholders present in this use case from supplier to accounting and from manufacturing to shipping and from quality assurance to wholesale and retail customers. The reconciliation of data usually occurs by a limited number of parties. Usually, the product's owner initiates the process and each departmental unit would collect their data to pass it on to a requesting department or authority.

The nature of value depends on which supply chain we are talking about. For example, shipping raw material from one party to another should be considered as value transfer of tangible products and shipping product designs should be consider as value transfer of intangible products (e.g. Intellectual Property of work, procedures & services)

However, the immutability of records depends on the application of the use case. If the supply chain is about rare arts and collectibles then it would make sense to keep an immutable record of transactions to counter forgery. But, if it is for daily ordinary purposes like who ships the package to customers, we may want to delete/refresh the ledger more often.

It is clear that blockchain for supply chain would yield a better solution. It can help us digitize the supply chain process, track the origins of a product and report on its quality during the shipment. We can use it to track the paper trails of shipping containers, reduce time spent in transit and shipping process, enhance transparency and security of product information exchanged between parties, reduce costs and complexity, improve stock management and reduce frauds and errors on the quality and quantity of products.

However, there are a few challenges involved in such a solution – public blockchain has a throughput problem where supply chain needs thousands of transactions per second with millions of users. We need to pay and incentivize the participation. It is likely that the private blockchain will have network problems as the size will be limited and the access of data will become somehow centralized. We also need to be vigilant of regulatory frameworks of all the geographies of stake holders. For example, it would be fine to ship wine and alcohol out of a port in China but it is a punishable crime in most Muslim countries like Saudi Arabia and Iran. All stakeholders need to agree on a single set of regulatory framework for the blockchain, or at least the set that goes from point A to point B, to be able to successfully run the process.

A blockchain-based solution running smart contracts works well with public blockchain by using the consensus protocol to "verify" the state of affairs achieved through validators and reporters to confirm the transaction and trigger the ending set of commands like making payments. For public blockchain it would also need "Value Tokens" to incentivize the validators, reporters and nodes who are working on consensus.

In this case, all stakeholders of the supply chain are going to use this application from suppliers to manufacturers and from shipping company to end consumers. The stakeholders need to adjust to this distributed command-and-control mechanism and don't have to wait for the centralized instructions to carry out their part of the plan. For example, a cloth supplier for undergarments can ship the cloth without worrying about ribbons or availability of other items of the supply chain needed to complete the product. He will also get paid for his services sooner as he is no more dependent on things he can't control. This autonomy will increase traceability, efficiency, productivity, transparency, provenance, trust and loyalty throughout the supply chain – processes, technology and people.

~~~~~

Use Case – DAO and Crime-as-a-Service

Decentralized Autonomous Organizations (DAO) is an organization that is completely defined online with all its rules and regulations written in smart contracts. It can hire humans to do the work it cannot do itself and can pay them through their internal capital. The tasks can be defined by participants in the DAO through votes. As Don and Alex Tapscott have mentioned in their book Blockchain Revolution[173], DAO can increase speed and reduce costs for businesses such as the expense of searching for talent, contracting, coordination and building or rebuilding trust.

DAO is a heavenly state for the preachers of open-society and the everything-transparent enthusiast. Where autonomy removes the labor of menial tasks from the periphery, the DAO attacks the core and removes the hierarchy, bureaucracy, and red tape from above. On the outset, it is a much needed and desirable state for all. But a deeper look can reveal the inherent dangers and consequences of DAO in practice.

Let's take a step back and see why we would like to replace the existing centralized systems – almost everything we do in our daily lives is centralized, from bank accounts to government taxation, from immigration to police, from money transfers to real-estate deeds and from personal wills to the entire democratic process. The current centralized system offers multiple disadvantages like privacy concerns, corruption at all levels or simply deceit and accidental or intentional loss of data (someone wiping off the entire bank's database). To avoid these problems and improve upon them, we seek DLT (Distributed Ledger Technology) with blockchain, where we can trust the un-trusted through algorithmic consensus verified by a cryptographic proof/work. DAO is a mechanism to realize this approach but it can backfire by the virtue of its very design that we all strive for. For example, in case of a fraud or default, how do you make someone responsible when DAO has unknown creators? If we consider DAO as a property and punish it, then why would the participants of DAO be punished for the crimes they have never committed (a bug in the code?). And how about the sociological underpinnings that arise because of DAO, as described by T. Gillespie in Relevance of Algorithms[174], such as patterns of inclusion, cycles of anticipation, evaluation of relevance, promise of algorithmic objectivity, production of calculated publics and entanglement with practice.

Let's look at some examples for businesses, governments and criminal organizations.

For business, it has a strong positive case in general, where the whole organization would be working as a self-organized swarm system (as we have flocks of birds or schools of fish in nature) where autonomous parts/roles of the organization can contract the work out to individual participants and workers on blockchain and bind them through smart contracts. For example, we can see an example of a bank giving a loan to build a house - it can contract the house building work to multiple contractors from painting to labor and from carpenter to blacksmith – once the individual players satisfy the state/work requirements, the money would automatically release to their respective accounts. We can place a complete supply-chain of our products on blockchain (as one company Provenance is doing). While it offers great transparency and financial fiduciary oversight, it can expose business secrets and cost margins to public in open, it can also attract hackers and malicious users to trick the system for corporate espionage and data breach.

For governments, DAO is a hard case to prove either way. On the one hand, it is good to remove the bottlenecks and disadvantages of a closed-centralized system and offer transparency, but on the other side, there are a lot of things in governments that cannot be open, i.e. those related to state secrets and strategic and military advances over enemies. Carrying out these processes though DAO will call for unwanted attention from both friends and foe.

For criminal organizations and drug cartels, DAO is the best thing that comes from the sky. They can maintain the loosely coupled control they all want (in case of arrest) so others can carry forward the organization and it would make it very hard to prove any wrong doing by a specific person in the eyes of court. In the paper, Ring of Gyges[175], the authors have presented a case of Crime-As-A-Service and it is pretty much a clear strategy to do illicit activities on blockchain using DAO and be less vulnerable to existing policing and law enforcement systems. We have the examples of SilkRoad[176], DAEMON, Beaver[177] and other Darknet marketplaces[178] that would deal with illicit drugs and criminal activities without the fear of getting caught. Far greater surveillance and regulations are needed for DAO when it comes to criminal activities.

One thing that stands out is the jurisdiction of DAO. Businesses, governments and crimes operate in certain geography with their own local laws and rules; one thing might be illegal in one place and completely legal in another place. DAO by design is a borderless organization and it would be a challenge to keep it under law for adjudication. We need to define a universal law for DAO before we can move further.

~~~~~

Use Case - Last Mile Problem in Developing Countries

"Last Mile Problem" is a metaphorical example to describe the delivery of goods and services to customers' premises. The *last mile* is the final leg of the delivery mechanism whether it is postal mail through postman on a bicycle, pizza delivery, internet connection though coax cables, cable TV, power/water supply or a wireless connection. Last mile is usually the most difficult, expensive, complex and hard-to-upgrade leg of the system. Think of it as a tree where the operation infrastructure is a big trunk while all the end users are the leaves at the edges. It is easier to upgrade the first or middle part (coax to fiber optic or bicycle to aircraft for example), it is very hard to upgrade the last mile and meet thousands of complex set of devices, regulations, geography and personal preferences at the end point. In technology, a small improvement in the last mile can increase the user adoption and satisfaction by many folds. This problem is not specific to digital currencies or least developed countries; rather it is a general problem and can be compared to any technology or non-technological solutions in the developing or developed world.

Point-of-Sale solution of cryptocurrency for non-crypto-aware population (close to 6.9 billion people) is the right way to start. Abra[179] is doing just that. It provides a multi-currency way in 50 countries to send and receive any combination of crypto or fiat currencies on the fly. It also allows any user to become a teller (think of Airbnb for money transfers). EasyPaisa[180] in Pakistan is doing the same with mobile enabled payments where anyone can use his/her mobile to make the payments for utility bills or to transfer money to their loved ones. EasyPaisa has 50% penetration in Pakistan; compare it with 12% of total banked population of the country. MPesa[181] is doing the same in Kenya and India while others are trying to achieve the same with lightning network[182]. However, one has to be very vigilant about the claims and services - we have seen many companies disappear after making big claims and raising a good amount of money, like CamelGram and ChangeTip.

Besides the last mile problem, there exist few other problems unique to least developed countries, for example regulatory mechanisms, world sanctions (AML, KYC, FATF due to terrorism financing or money laundering sanctions on certain countries), and geo-political circumstances (Nike, for example, weren't able to provide running shoes to Iran's FIFA World Cup team due to US restrictions[183]). Additionally, there is the issue of a country's unique capital controls and regulation of entry and exit points of wealth, as with the case of Argentine, Greece, Venezuela, China, India etc., and simply the unavailability of the latest technology to provide the service (satellite location services, internet over power lines etc.) These issues can and should be considered as opportunities in least developed countries to innovate and deliver the best to the people who deserve the most to improve their lives, health and well-being.

~~~~~

Use Case – Sharia-Compliant Cryptocurrencies for "Unbanked" and "Unbitcoined"

From the start, digital currencies like BitCoin, Ethereum and others have gained the attraction of bad guys for their illicit businesses. We have seen the examples of Silk Road[184] (United States Versus Ross Ulbricht) and Terrorism Financing (Long Island Versus Zoobia Shehnaz[185]). The free and unchecked flow of digital currencies in and out of a country poses a security risk for the country in particular and for the world in general. Terrorists can use it to channelize their funding campaigns and attract new recruits by paying them anonymously. Since digital currency remittance can come from any part of the planet, it would create a global risk.

There is also the possibility of tax evasion by corporates or ordinary citizens of the country who wish to send their black-money off-shore to hide it from tax authorities of their respective governments. We have seen this practice again and again; it was the reason behind the big political uproar recently after the Panama Papers leak[186].

Then there is "Hundi" or "Hawala" scheme, where one person would send remittances' reference to some other country without following the legal procedure or transferring any money through the banking channel; the receiving party would receive it in digital currency and cash it out in the local market, thus affecting the flight of money in and out of country and bypassing the current money caps and limits we have for foreign and local reserves.

Digital currencies can also aid regulations arbitrage, when one takes the money for something that is illegal in one jurisdiction and allowed in another. For example, selling of marijuana would be considered perfectly fine in Germany while it is a crime in the US. People can use the free flow of digital currencies remittances for a country to make it the financial hub of crypto-crimes all over the world in no time.

Situations like these call for strict rules and regulations which manifest in the form of anti-money-laundering (AML), counter-terrorism financing (CTF), and know-your-customer (KYC) laws. It has the ability to suffocate day-to-day financial operations and free will of customers of a given country. Governments all over the world are campaigning for cashless societies and "banked-population" to have greater visibility of day-to-day financial affairs of their citizens.

On the other hand, approximately 38% of the world's adults, i.e. 2 billion people[187], do not have bank accounts for various reasons. All these people, primarily, and many other "banked" people frequently do their daily transactions in cash. India, China and Indonesia account for 40% of the "unbanked" population while another 17% comes from Sub-Saharan Africa[188].

Globally cash transactions account for 63% ($11.84 trillion) of overall transactions. The cash-less electronic transactions in OECD countries are close to 67% while in South Asia it is only 14% of total transactions[189].

There are several reasons for dealing in cash. Cash requires no paperwork while doing transactions and therefore is very fast. It also provides anonymity, a prime requirement for illicit activities like drug, human and sex trafficking. One study finds 90% of currency notes in circulation in America with traces of drugs on it[190]. Criminals and war lords move approximately $2 trillion across borders in cash every year[191].

Cash has its own set of problems. First it is highly insecure, once you lose it or it gets snatched from you, there is very little hope to retrieve it back. It is heavy for large amounts - a million dollar can weight up to 22 pounds in weight[192]. And more often than not, it attracts criminals. The cash economy is largely un-documented, making it very hard to access, plan, budget and forecast. How do governments plan for financial well-being of its citizens when they do not know the size of the total market? Cash economy also deprives governments for their due share of taxes that can be then used for public goods, infrastructure and defense needs[193].

Financial inclusion through banks comes with its own challenges like lengthy paper work and hefty fees for financial services. Mobile banking or digital financial solutions come in handy and provide the best of the both worlds – on the one hand, they provide a documented way for the economy to be monitored, grow and forecast, and on the other hand it requires very less paperwork (as most countries already have KYC and AML measures in place for issuance of mobile SIMs), making it possible for all individuals with mobile bank account and their transactions to be traced back. Digital currencies can also provide a complete ledger of all the transactions back and forth for the currency in question.

Countries have been trying to get rid of the cash economy all together. There are a few economists in America lobbying to remove $50 and $100 notes from general circulation[194]. Singapore eliminated the $10,000 note in 2014[195]. Sweden is gradually removing ATM machines from rural villages[196]. South Korea is all set to make the country cash-less by 2020[197]. France has banned any transactions in cash for more than 1,000 pounds[198]. Venezuela has removed the 100 bolivar note[199] and Europe is going to kill their 500 pound note from this year[200]. Greece has banned all citizens from keeping more than 15,000 pounds cash in their possession[201].

United Nations, with the support of Bill and Melinda Gates Foundation, Master Card, Citi Bank, For Foundation, Omidyar Network, USAID and others, has launched BetterThanCash[202] Alliance and the United Nations Capital Development Fund has been working on MM4P (Mobile Money for the Poor)[203] initiative to bring cashless transactions to 2 billion unbanked adults in the world.

Access to financial instruments will bring trust, equal opportunity, gender balance, employment, health and literacy to the poor people of the world and will restrict criminal activities[204].

The same laws and regulations for identity requirements that are restricting people to use traditional banking services are in practice to push them away from digital currencies in one form or another, for better or worse, for the exact same reasons – to barter their financial privacy against banking services.

Islamic banking can fill this gap and offer a principle-based ethical alternative.

There are 1.6 billion Muslims in the world. Muslim countries contribute about 9% of the global GDP and Islamic banking assets are close to US$3 trillion. Islamic banking is functional and thriving in 60 countries worldwide. Islamic banking progress is steady and did not collapse with global financial crisis of 2008. Anything that would attract the attention of these people and financial institutions would guarantee some portion of success.

Islam does not allow the functions of banking that rely on Riba (Interest), Gharar (Uncertainty or Excessive Risk), or impressible businesses like alcohol, sex, drugs and gambling etc. Cryptocurrencies are based on consensus algorithms (PoW, PoS, PoST etc.) instead of centralized-interest-based fiat.

Cryptocurrencies are closer to Islam than fiat. Sharia-compliant cryptocurrencies would attract the religious and practicing Muslims worldwide to benefit from this new form of money and the underlying distributed ledger technology.

Due to legal boundaries set by Islamic principles of banking and businesses, it is very costly and laborious to form the agreement among various parties. Moving everything on blockchain-based smart contract would save time, resources and simplify the process of Islamic banking manifolds. Islamic smart contracts are the need of the time for Islamic finance that solve the exact problem that Islamic banking has been struggling with for decades.

The concept of sharia-compliant cryptocurrencies will take its time to go mainstream. Islamic banking is a very small portion of the global banking system. However, we can see some recent progress like IMF adopting the core principles of Islamic banking[205], adding it to their 2019 reporting category[206], SettleMint helping Islamic Development Bank[207], or blockchain adoption inside UAE, but the claim that sharia-compliant cryptocurrencies can speed up the progress as if on steroids is a tall one.

Cryptocurrencies, by virtue of their programmability, provide an added and somewhat historically missing element to the concept of money. Money is (just) a medium-of-exchange, it does not understand or complain when put to bad use like assassination, drug, sex and human trafficking, ransom or war etc.

Islamic law is more concerned with the morality of financial transactions rather than the form and shape of the money being used. Where the token is driving its value from is more important in Islamic jurisprudence than the token itself. If the "value" is driven from permissible means and functions in Islam, it is valid, if the "value" comes from function or processes deem forbidden in Islam, it is impermissible. With the evolution of cryptocurrencies we can have ethically aware, conscious money where the Islamic principles of its usage can be coded inside the money.

Sharia-compliant cryptocurrencies would not only increase the market share of crypto users but also can provide an alternative way to move people from "unbanked" to "banked" and from "unbitcoined" to "bitcoined" while keeping the law of the land intact through its principle-based architecture and design.

~~~~~

Recommended Books

1.   History of Money: Financial History: From Barter to Bitcoin - An Overview of Our Economic History, Monetary System & Currency Crisis by Mike Thornton
2.   How Global Currencies Work: Past, Present, and Future by Barry Eichengreen
3.   The History of Money: From Bartering to Banking by Martin Jenkins
4.   The History of Money by Jack Weatherford
5.   The Age of Cryptocurrency: How Bitcoin and the Blockchain Are Challenging the Global Economic Order by Paul Vigna
6.   Money: The Unauthorized Biography – From Coinage to Cryptocurrencies by Felix Martin
7.   Blockchain Revolution: How the Technology Behind Bitcoin and Other Cryptocurrencies Is Changing the World by Don Tapscott and Alex Tapscott
8.   Digital Gold: Bitcoin and the Inside Story of the Misfits and Millionaires Trying to Reinvent Money by Nathaniel Popper
9.   A History of Digital Currency in the United States: New Technology in an Unregulated Market (Palgrave Advances in the Economics of Innovation and Technology) by P. Carl Mullan
10.   Blockchain For Dummies by Tiana Laurence
11.   Bitcoin For Dummies by Prypto
12.   Cryptoassets: The Innovative Investor's Guide to Bitcoin and Beyond by Chris Burniske
13.   Naked Money: A Revealing Look at Our Financial System by Charles Wheelan
14.   Bits to Bitcoin: How Our Digital Stuff Works (The MIT Press) by Mark Stuart Day
15.   The Basics of Bitcoins and Blockchains: An Introduction to Cryptocurrencies and the Technology that Powers Them by Antony Lewis

16. Capitalism without Capital: The Rise of the Intangible Economy by Jonathan Haskel
17. A Cultural History of Money: Volumes 1-6 (The Cultural Histories Series) by Bill Maurer
18. Building Blockchain Projects: Building decentralized Blockchain applications with Ethereum and Solidity by Narayan Prusty
19. Cryptocurrencies simply explained - by TenX Co-Founder Dr. Julian Hosp
20. The History of Money for Understanding Economics by Vincent Lannoye
21. Dark Money: The Hidden History of the Billionaires Behind the Rise of the Radical Right by Jane Mayer
22. A History of Money: From Ancient Times to the Present Day by Glyn Davies
23. Life After Google: The Fall of Big Data and the Rise of the Blockchain Economy by George Gilder
24. Ethereum For Dummies by Tiana Laurence
25. Mastering Ethereum: Building Smart Contracts and DApps by Andreas M. Antonopoulos
26. Blockchain By Example: Decentralized applications using Bitcoin, Ethereum, and Hyperledger by Bellaj Badr
27. Confessions of a Microfinance Heretic by Hugh Sinclair
28. Seduced and Betrayed: Exposing the Contemporary Microfinance Phenomenon by Milford Bateman
29. Investigating Cryptocurrencies: Understanding, Extracting, and Analyzing Blockchain Evidence by Nick Furneaux
30. Solidity Programming Essentials: A beginner's guide to build smart contracts for Ethereum and blockchain by Ritesh Modi
31. A History of Central Banking & The Enslavement of Mankind by Stephen Mitford Goodson
32. Social by Nature: The Promise and Peril of Sociogenomics by Catherine Bliss
33. Prosperity without Growth: Foundations for the Economy of Tomorrow by Tim Jackson

34.   Managing Innovation: Integrating Technological, Market and Organizational Change by Joe Tidd

35.   The Ascent of Money: A Financial History of the World by Niall Ferguson

36.   Blockchain and the Law: The Rule of Code by Primavera De Filippi

37.   Blockchain: A Practical Guide to Developing Business, Law, and Technology Solutions by Joseph J. Bambara

38.   The Book of Satoshi: The Collected Writings of Bitcoin Creator Satoshi Nakamoto by Phil Champagne

39.   Art of the Initial Coin Offering: Lessons Learned from the Launch of a Crypto-Token by Andrew James Chapin

40.   Bible: The Ultimate Guide About Blockchain, Mining, Trading, ICO, Ethereum Platform, Exchanges, Top Cryptocurrencies for Investing and Perfect Strategies to Make Money by Alan T. Norman

41.   Attack of the 50 Foot Blockchain: Bitcoin, Blockchain, Ethereum & Smart Contracts by David Gerard

42.   Blockchain: Uncovering Blockchain Technology, Cryptocurrencies, Bitcoin and the Future of Money: Blockchain and Cryptocurrency Exposed (Blockchain and Cryptocurrency as the Future of Money) (Volume 1) by Alan Wright

43.   Blockchain: Trust Companies: Every Company Is at Risk of Being Disrupted by a Trusted Version of Itself by Richie Etwaru

44.   Blockchain Basics: A Non-Technical Introduction in 25 Steps by Daniel Drescher

~~~~~

References:

[1] Glyn Davies, "A History of Money: From Ancient Times to the Present Day", University of Wales Press, 3rd edition (November 2002)

[2] Catherine Eagleton and Jonathan Williams, "Money: A History", British Museum Press, 2nd Revised ed. (December 31, 2007)

[3] Glyn Davies and Duncan Connors, "A History of Money", University of Wales Press, 4th Edition (July 15, 2016)

[4] David Graeber, "Debt - Updated and Expanded: The First 5,000 Years", Melville House; Updated, Expanded edition (October 28, 2014)

[6] Catherine Eagleton and Jonathan Williams, "Money: A History", British Museum Press, 2nd Revised ed.(December 31, 2007

[7] Glyn Davies and Duncan Connors, "History of Money", University of Wales Press, 4th Edition (July 15, 2016)

[8] Jack Weatherford, "The History of Money" Crown Business, Reprint edition (September 22, 2009)

[9] Kathryn E. Slanski, *The Law of Hammurabi and Its Audience*, 24 Yale J.L. & Human. 97 (2012); J.G. Manning, *The Representation of Justice in Ancient Egypt*, 24 Yale J.L. & Human. 111 (201

[10] Edwin Black, "Banking on Baghdad: Inside Iraq's 7,000-Year History of War, Profit, and Conflict", John Wiley & Sons Inc.; 1 edition (October 4, 2004)

[11] Jack Weatherford, "The History of Money" Crown Business, Reprint edition (September 22, 2009)

[12] Niall Ferguson Penguin, "The Ascent of Money: A Financial History of the World", Penguin Books, 1st edition (October 27, 2009)

[13] Milton Friedman, "Money Mischief: Episodes in Monetary History", Mariner Books, 1st edition (March 31, 1994)

[14] Mike Thornton, "History: History of Money: Financial History: From Barter to Bitcoin - An Overview of Our: Economic History, Monetary System, & Currency Crisis",

[15] Felix Martin, "Money: The Unauthorized Biography--From Coinage to Cryptocurrencies", Vintage, Reprint edition (January 6, 2015)

[16] Murray N. Rothbard, "A History of Money and Banking in the United States: The Colonial Era to World War II" Ludwig Von Mises Inst, 1st edition

[17] Martin Jenkins and Satoshi Kitamura, "Illustrator The History of Money: From Bartering to Banking", Candlewick, Reprint edition (September 22, 2015)

Du Plessis, S. (2012). A stone under the ocean: How money did not disappear and what we now need to do about it. Biennial South African Reserve Bank Conference Proceedings. Pretoria: South African Reserve Bank

[19] Goldstein, Jacob; Kestenbaum, David. "The Island of Stone Money", [Online] 2010.

[20] Satoshi Nakamoto. "Bitcoin: A Peer-to-Peer Electronic Cash System", [Online] 2008.

[21] Li, T., Ji, J., Zhou, Z. et al. Archaeol Anthropol Sci (2017) 9: 395. https://doi.org/10.1007/s12520-015-0293-9

[22] Peranson, Mark. 2008. First You Get the Power, Then You Get the Money: Two Models of Film Festivals. In *Dekalog 3: On Film Festivals*, ed. Richard Porton, 37. London: Wallflower.

[23] Cipolla, Carlo. 1982. The Monetary Policy of Fourteenth-Century Florence. Berkeley: University of California Press.

[24] Marco Polo and Ronald Latham, "The Travels of Marco Polo", Penguin Classics; Reissue edition (September 30, 1958)

[25] G. Edward Griffin, "The Creature from Jekyll Island : A Second Look at the Federal Reserve", Amer Media, 3rd edition (May 1998)

[26] DK, "How Money Works: The Facts Visually Explained (How Things Work)", March 14, 2017

[27] Yanis Varoufakis and Jacob Moe, "Talking to My Daughter About the Economy: or, How Capitalism Works--and How It Fails", Farrar, Straus and Giroux (May 8, 2018)

[28] Jane Mayer, "Dark Money: The Hidden History of the Billionaires Behind the Rise of the Radical Right", (January 24, 2017)

[29] Levitt, Steven, D., and John A. List. 2007. "What Do Laboratory Experiments Measuring Social Preferences Reveal About the Real World?" Journal of Economic Perspectives, 21 (2): 153-174. DOI: 10.1257/jep.21.2.153

[30] Irwin, D. A (2013), 'The Nixon Shock after Forty Years: The Import Surcharge Revisited', World Trade Review, 12(1): 29–56

[31] JR Behrman, "International commodity agreements: an evaluation of the unctad Integrated Commodity Programme"

[32] Steven Bryan, "The Gold Standard at the Turn of the Twentieth Century: Rising Powers, Global Money, and the Age of Empire", Columbia Studies in International and Global History, Aug 31, 2010

[33] https://en.wikipedia.org/wiki/National_debt_of_the_United_States

[34] https://bigthink.com/paul-ratner/the-us-spent-56-trillion-on-war-since-911

[35] Paul Brest and Hal Harvey, "Money Well Spent", Bloomberg Press (November 28, 2008)

[36] Chivian D, Brodie EL, Alm EJ, Culley DE, Dehal PS, et al. (2008) Environmental genomics reveals a single-species ecosystem deep within Earth. Science 322: 275–278

[37] https://www.nytimes.com/2017/07/25/world/asia/afghanistan-trump-mineral-deposits.html

[38] https://www.economist.com/asia/1998/08/20/pakistan-takes-a-beating

[39] https://en.wikipedia.org/wiki/Hungarian_peng%C5%91

[40] https://blockgeeks.com/

[41] https://www.coindesk.com/6-3-billion-2018-ico-funding-already-outpaced-2017/

[42] https://www.coindesk.com/ico-tracker/

[43] Dror Futter, Blockchain Law: ICO Regulation and Other Legal Considerations in the Blockchain Ecosystem The Journal of PLI, Press, Vol. 2, No. 1, Winter 2018 - Page 21 - (© 2018 Practicing Law Institute)

[44] Eduardo da Cruz Rodrigues e Silva, Legal Framework of Initial Coin Offerings, Master's Thesis, Program Law, specialization law and technology, Tallin 2018

[45] Anthony R.G. Nolan, Edward T. Dartley, Mary Burke Baker, John ReVeal, Judith E. Rinearson, "Initial coin offerings: key U.S. legal considerations for ICO investors and sponsors", Journal of Investment Compliance, https://doi.org/10.1108/, JOIC-02-2018-0016

[46] SEC ICO

[47] European Parliament Laws on Crypto Assets

[48] EU Warnings on ICO

[49] Securities and Exchange Commission, SECURITIES EXCHANGE ACT OF 1934, Release No. 81207 / July 25, 2017 Report of Investigation Pursuant to Section 21(a) of the Securities Exchange Act of 1934: The DAO

[50] 328 U.S. 293, 301 (1946); see also United Housing Found., Inc. v. Forman, 421 U.S. 837, 852–53 (1975). Other standards may apply to the characterization of a token under the Securities Act depending on the characteristics of the token. See, e.g., Reves v. Ernst & Young, 494 U.S. 56 (1990).

[51] EVA TOMÁŠKOVÁ — DAVID SEHNÁLEK, The Hierarchy of Legal Sources – Relation between International Treaties Concluded with Third States by the EU and by the Member States

[52] Report of Investigation Pursuant to Section 21 of the Securities Act.

[53] Rule 506, Regulation D

[54] General Solicitation Rule 506 C

[55] US Commodity and Exchange Act

[56] US SEC Laws

[57] EU Security and Market Authority

[58] World Bank Working Group White Paper # 184, Tanja Boskovic, Caroline Cerruti and Michel Noel, Comparing European and U.S. Securities Regulations

[59] FCA Framework and Warnings for the ICO

[60] SAFT Framework

[61] SEC Rule 105b – Anti Fraud

[62] Investment Advisor Act 1940

[63] BSA – Bank Secrecy Act

[64] Money Transmitter License

[65] US CryptoCurrency Tax Fairness Bill

[66] N. Szabo. (1994). *Smart Contracts*. [Online]. Available:http://szabo.best.vwh.net/smart.contracts.html
[67] http://thebusinessblockchain.com/

[68] https://bitcoinmagazine.com/articles/the-blockchain-developer-shortage-emerging-trends-and-perspectives-1477930838/

[69] https://www.ccn.com/40-trillion-cryptocurrency-market-cap-definitely-possible-pantera-capital-ceo/

[70] https://www.computerworld.com/article/3235972/it-careers/blockchain-jobs-continue-to-explode-offer-salary-premiums.html

[71] https://hackernoon.com/become-a-blockchain-developer-and-get-rich-74712f1dd310

[72] https://techcrunch.com/2018/02/14/blockchain-engineers-are-in-demand/
[73] https://blocktribe.com/

[74] https://www.ted.com/talks/neha_narula_the_future_of_money

75

https://www.ted.com/talks/don_tapscott_how_the_blockchain_is_changing_mone
y_and_business

76

https://www.ted.com/talks/rachel_botsman_we_ve_stopped_trusting_institutions_
and_started_trusting_strangers

77 https://www.ted.com/watch/ted-institute/ted-bcg/blockchain-and-the-middleman

78

https://www.ted.com/talks/paul_kemp_robertson_bitcoin_sweat_tide_meet_the_f
uture_of_branded_currency
79 https://www.ted.com/talks/mike_schwartz_the_potential_of_blockchain

80

https://www.ted.com/talks/bettina_warburg_how_the_blockchain_will_radically_tr
ansform_the_economy

81 https://hbr.org/2017/01/the-truth-about-blockchain

82 https://dci.mit.edu/

83 http://www.oxfordblockchain.net/

84 https://digitalchamber.org/

85 https://www.r3.com/

86 https://www.hyperledger.org/

87 https://new.consensys.net/

88 https://www.blockchainresearchinstitute.org/

89 https://www-01.ibm.com/common/ssi/cgi-bin/ssialias?htmlfid=XIM12354USEN

90 https://smtebooks.com/Downloads/4787/mastering-blockchain-pdf

91 https://bravenewcoin.com/assets/Reference-Papers/A-Gentle-Introduction/A-
Gentle-Introduction-To-Blockchain-Technology-WEB.pdf

92 https://unglueit-
files.s3.amazonaws.com/ebf/05db7df4f31840f0a873d6ea14dcc28d.pdf

93 http://manuals.makeuseof.com.s3.amazonaws.com/for-
mobile/MakeUseOf.com_-_BitCoin_Guide.pdf

94 https://gitcoin.co/

[95] Darwin, C. *On the Origin of Species by Means of Natural Selection, or the Preservation of Favoured Races in the Struggle for Life.* London: John Murray, modern reprint Charles Darwin, Julian Huxley (2003) "On The Origin of Species" Signet Classics. ISBN 0-451-52906-5

[96] Bisq – The P2P Exchange Network. (accessed 17 February 2018) https://bisq.network/

[97] No Author. "DHS Says Darknet Criminals Are Switching From Bitcoin to Monero." *Deep Dot Web* (accessed 15 February 2018) https://www.deepdotweb.com/2017/09/20/dhs-says-darknet-criminals-switching-bitcoin-monero/

[98] PERRY P. "What Killed off the Neanderthals? You Might Not Like the Answer." *Big Think* (accessed 17 February 2018) http://bigthink.com/philip-perry/guess-what-killed-off-the-neanderthals-you-might-not-like-the-answer

[99] Darwin, C. (1917). The Origin of Species by Means of Natural Selection.

[100] Kakushadze, Z., & Kyung-Soo Liew, J. (2018). CryptoRuble: From Russia with Love. Retrieved from CryptoRuble: From Russia with Love Risk, January 2018, pp. 53-54 20 Pages Posted: 26 Oct 2017 Last revised: 17 Jan 2018 Zura Kakushadze Quantigic Solutions LLC; Free University of Tbilisi Jim Kyung-Soo Liew Johns Hopkins University - Carey Business Scho.

[101] Lu, D. L. (2018, March). Bitcoin: speculative bubble, financial risk and regulatory response. Retrieved from Butterworths Journal of International Banking and Financial Law: https://www.researchgate.net/profile/Lerong_Lu/publication/323874289_Bitcoin_Speculative_Bubble_Financial_Risk_and_Regulatory_Response/links/5ab0fb0aa6fdcc1bc0bee3b6/Bitcoin-Speculative-Bubble-Financial-Risk-and-Regulatory-Response.pdf

[102] Proteous, D. (2006). Banking and the Last Mile: Technology and the Distribution of Financial Services in Developing Countries. World Bank.

[103] Sawson, T. (2015). Consensus-as-a-service: a brief report on the emergence of permissioned, distributed ledger systems.

[104] McElroy K. "Symbiosis: when living together is win-win" *Cosmos* (accessed 17 February 2018) https://cosmosmagazine.com/social-sciences/symbiosis-when-living-together-win-win

[105] Marr B."5 Blockchain Opportunities No Company Can Afford To Miss" *Forbes* (accessed 17 February 2018)

https://www.forbes.com/sites/bernardmarr/2018/02/07/5-blockchain-opportunities-no-company-can-afford-to-miss

[106] Bull, G. (2018, May 29). Blockchain: A Solution in Search of a Problem? Retrieved from Consultative Group to Assist the Poor: http://www.cgap.org/blog/blockchain-solution-search-problem

[107] No Author. "What is Ransomware?" *Trend Micro USA* (accessed 17 February 2018) https://www.trendmicro.com/vinfo/us/security/definition/ransomware

[108] Prisco G. Plantoids: The First Blockchain-Based Artificial Life Forms. *Bitcoin Magazine* (accessed 17 February 2018) https://bitcoinmagazine.com/articles/plantoids-the-first-blockchain-based-artificial-life-forms-1482768916/

[109] Nínive Aguiar Colonello, Klaus Hartfelder. She's my girl - male accessory gland products and their function in the reproductive biology of social bees. s.l.: Apidologie, Springer Verlag, 2005

[110] Wolfner M. F. "Tokens of love: Functions and regulation of drosophila male accessory gland products." *Elsevier* 27.3 179-192 (1997) doi: 10.1016/S0965-1748(96)00084-7 https://doi.org/10.1016/S0965-1748(96)00084-7

[111] https://en.wikipedia.org/wiki/Russian_interference_in_the_2016_United_States_elections

[112] https://www.theguardian.com/uk-news/2018/mar/26/cambridge-analytica-trump-campaign-us-election-laws

[113] https://www.apnews.com/6c686219242c48c1b9a2653a4972a3c3

[114] https://www.theguardian.com/world/2018/jan/02/us-silent-as-honduras-protesters-killed-in-post-election-violence

[115] http://www.dailymail.co.uk/news/article-5628475/We-watching-Political-killings-shake-Mexico-election.html

[116] http://time.com/85535/ten-killed-in-assam-attacks/

[117] https://tribune.com.pk/story/719730/electoral-fraud-nadra-finds-rigging-in-records-of-na-118/

[118] https://www.dawn.com/news/795310

[119] https://www.dawn.com/news/1048088

[120] https://www.ted.com/talks/pia_mancini_how_to_upgrade_democracy_for_the_internet_era

[121] http://democracyos.org/

[122] http://votewatcher.com/#voting

[123] https://voteunits.com/?/

[124] https://www.democracy.earth/

[125] http://votosocial.github.io/

[126] https://followmyvote.com/

[127] https://www.agora.vote/

[128] https://www.theregister.co.uk/2018/03/21/no_sierra_leone_did_not_run_the_worlds_first_blockchain_election/

[129] https://techcrunch.com/2018/02/24/liquid-democracy-uses-blockchain/

[130] https://united.vote/

[131] https://patents.google.com/patent/US9836908B2/

[132] http://freeandfair.us/

[133] https://voatz.com/

[134] https://www.brookings.edu/blog/techtank/2018/05/30/how-blockchain-could-improve-election-transparency/

[135] https://votem.com/

[136] https://www.economist.com/asia/2018/01/11/a-watertight-store-of-indians-personal-data-proves-leaky

[137] https://www.techjuice.pk/nadra-police-telcos-citizens-data-being-sold-publicly-facebook/

[138] https://www.zastrin.com/

[139] https://www.zastrin.com/simple-ethereum-voting-dapp.html

[140] http://solidity.readthedocs.io/en/v0.4.24/solidity-by-example.html

[141] Lynn Parramore, "$MeToo: The Economic Cost of Sexual Harassment", https://www.ineteconomics.org/research/research-papers/metoo-the-economic-cost-of-sexual-harassment, accessed on April 19, 2018 10:30 AM

[142] ERC, "The Cost of Sexual Harassment in the Workplace", https://www.yourerc.com/blog/post/the-cost-of-sexual-harassment-in-the-workplace.aspx, accessed on April 19, 2018, 11:00 AM

[143] Bill Fotsch and John Case, "The Terrible Cost Of Sexual Harassment--And How To Avoid It", Forbes, https://www.forbes.com/sites/fotschcase/2018/01/23/the-terrible-cost-of-sexual-harassment-and-how-to-avoid-it/ accessed on April 19, 2018 2:41 PM

[144] United States Congress, 2012, Is Brooklyn being counted? : Problems with the 2010 Census

[145] Alan, H. Peters and Heather, MacDonald 2005, Unlocking the Census with GIS, Esri Press

[146] Hinckley, Kathleen 2012, Your Guide to the Federal Census", Betterway Books

[147] Joe, R. Feagin, Clairece, Booher and Feagin R. 2011, Racial and Ethnic Relations, Census Update (9th Edition), Pearson

[148] Reynolds, Farley and John Haaga (Editors) 2000, The American People: Census 2000, Russell Sage Foundation Census Series

[149] William H. Frey 2011, Investigating Change: Web-based Analyses of US Census and American Community Survey Data 3rd Edition, Cengage Learning

[150] Swaroop S. R. 2018, Truth About Muslim Population Explosion in India: Evidence From Census 2011] Kindle Edition

[151] Abraham, Okolo 1999, The Nigerian Census: Problems and Prospects, The American Statistician, 53:4, 321-325

[152] Karim, Mehtab. October 17 2017, Missing People in Census, Daily DAWN, https://www.dawn.com/news/1364371 accessed on July 23, 2018 12:36 PM

[153] Israr, Faraz. November 6 2017, 15 million Karachiites missing in census, daily Nation, https://nation.com.pk/06-Nov-2017/15-million-karachiites-missing-in-census-claims-sattar accessed on July 23, 2018 12:37 pm

[154] CBS 2010, https://www.cbsnews.com/news/2010-census-missed-15-million-minorities/, accessed on July 23, 2018 12:44 PM

[155] Census Bureau, 2016, 2020 Census: Respondent Validation of Non-ID Processing in the 2020 Decennial Census, https://www.census.gov/programs-surveys/decennial-census/2020-census/planning-management/planning-docs/respondent_validation_non_id.html, accessed on July 23, 2018 12:46 PM

[156] Margo J. Anderson 2015, The American Census: A Social History, Second Edition, Yale University Press; 2 edition

[157] Maureen Kent 2015, Development of the 2020 Census: Selected Analyses and Issues (Economic Issues, Problems and Perspectives), Nova Science Pub, UK ed. Edition

[158] William J. Sutherland 2006, Ecological Census Techniques: A Handbook 2nd

Edition, Cambridge University Press

[159] Usmani, Zeeshan-ul-hassan 2018, Invisible BlockChain and Plasticity of Money – Adam Smith Meets Darwin to Buy Crypto Currency, Workshop on Blockchain and Smart Contract Technologi, Business Information Systems, Berlin, Germany, July 18, 2018.

[160] George Gilder, 2018, Life After Google: The Fall of Big Data and the Rise of the Blockchain Economy, Gateway Editions

[161] Daniel Drescher, 2017, Blockchain Basics: A Non-Technical Introduction in 25 Steps, APress, 1st ed.

[162] OHCHR 1989, Convention on the Rights of the Child, Adopted and opened for signature, ratification and accession by General Assembly resolution 44/25 of 20 November 1989,

[163] Don Tapscott and Alex Tapscott 2016, Blockchain Revolution: How the Technology Behind Bitcoin Is Changing Money, Business, and the World, Portfolio

[164] Paul Vigna and Michael J. Casey, 2018, The Truth Machine: The Blockchain and the Future of Everything, St. Martin's Press

[165] William H. Frey 2011, Investigating Change: Web-based Analyses of US Census and American Community Survey Data 3rd Edition, Cengage Learning

[166] Reynolds, Farley and John Haaga (Editors) 2000, The American People: Census 2000, Russell Sage Foundation Census Series

[167] Ivan, Canales. 2017 – Census based referendum, https://devpost.com/software/census-bye3lj#updates, accessed on July 23, 2018 12:13 PM

[168] NovaTeqni, Novus. 2017, http://novateqni.com/2017/10/31/novateqni-and-novus-to-showcase-new-blockchain-capable-census-devices/, accessed on July 23, 2018 10:49 AM

[169] World Economic Forum, 2017, The Value of Data, https://www.weforum.org/agenda/2017/09/the-value-of-data/, accessed on July 25, 2018, 2:43 PM

[170] Frank Vogel 2000,Studies in Islamic Law and Society, Islamic Law and Legal System: Studies of Saudi Arabia, Brill

[171] Hooker, M. B. 1978. A Concise Legal History of South-East Asia. Oxford: Clarendon Press

[172] Frank Vogel 2000,Studies in Islamic Law and Society, Islamic Law and Legal System: Studies of Saudi Arabia, Brill

[173] Blockchain Revolution: How the Technology Behind Bitcoin and Other Cryptocurrencies Is Changing the World by Don Tapscott and Alex Tapscott

[174] Gillespie TL. The relevance of algorithms. In: Gillespie TL, Bockzkowski P, Foot K, editors. Media
Technologies. Cambridge, MA, USA: MIT Press; forthcoming.

[175] A. Juels, A. Kosba, and E. Shi. The ring of gyges: Using smart contracts for crime. Manuscript, 2015.

[176] https://en.wikipedia.org/wiki/Silk_Road_(marketplace)

[177] https://www.deepdotweb.com/2016/05/28/honest-dark-net-market-ever/

[178] https://www.wired.com/2014/04/darkmarket/

[179] https://www.abra.com/

[180] https://www.easypaisa.com.pk/

[181] https://www.safaricom.co.ke/personal/m-pesa

[182] https://medium.com/@limexp/lightning-network-last-mile-solution-d3b9e29a0d1a

[183] http://www.espn.com/soccer/fifa-world-cup/story/3522512/nike-withdraws-iran-world-cup-squads-supply-of-boots-due-to-sanctions

[184] UNITED STATES OF AMERICA v. ROSS WILLIAM ULBRICHT DREAD PIRATE ROBERTS SILK ROAD SEALED DEFENDANT DPR

[185] https://www.justice.gov/usao-edny/pr/long-island-woman-indicted-bank-fraud-and-money-laundering-support-terrorists

[186] https://offshoreleaks.icij.org/

[187] https://globalfindex.worldbank.org/

[188] www.worldbank.org/content/dam/Worldbank/Research/.../PDF/N2Unbanked.pdf

[189] http://www.worldbank.org/en/news/press-release/2016/06/27/small-retailers-transact-19-trillion-in-cash-annually-new-world-economic-forum-and-world-bank-group-study-shows

[190] https://www.acs.org/content/acs/en/pressroom/newsreleases/2009/august/new-study-up-to-90-percent-of-us-paper-money-contains-traces-of-cocaine.html

[191] https://medium.com/war-is-boring/transnational-crime-made-a-trillion-dollars-in-2016-bd4a696ae635

[192] https://www.fivecentnickel.com/how-much-does-a-million-dollars-weigh/

[193] https://www.files.ethz.ch/isn/154325/Oct2012Moshi.pdf

[194] http://fortune.com/2016/06/17/100-bill/

[195] https://www.reuters.com/article/singapore-regulations/singapore-to-stop-issuing-s10000-banknote-to-prevent-money-laundering-idUSL4N0PD2M120140702

[196] http://business.financialpost.com/business-insider/people-in-sweden-are-hiding-cash-in-their-microwaves-because-of-a-fascinating-and-terrifying-economic-experiment

[197] https://bitrazzi.com/south-korea-to-go-cash-less-by-2020-thanks-to-blockchain-and-cryptocurrency/

[198] https://www.french-property.com/news/money_france/cash_payments_limits

[199] https://www.theguardian.com/world/2016/dec/13/venezuela-100-bolivar-bills-sudden-ban-colombia-nicolas-maduro

[200] https://www.nytimes.com/2016/05/05/business/international/ecb-to-remove-500-bill-the-bin-laden-bank-note-criminals.html

[201] https://www.reuters.com/article/us-eurozone-greece-capital-controls/greece-loosens-capital-controls-raises-cash-withdrawal-limit-idUSKCN1GC1KZ

[202] https://www.betterthancash.org/

[203] http://www.uncdf.org/fr/mm4p

[204] https://www.odi.org/resources/docs/6099.pdf

[205] https://www.imf.org/en/News/Articles/2018/05/24/pr18193imf-adopts-decisions-to-the-cpifr-for-banking

[206] https://www.reuters.com/article/us-islamic-finance-imf/imf-to-add-islamic-finance-to-market-surveillance-in-2019-idUSKCN1IQ081

[207] https://www.settlemint.com/project/2017/10/15/settlemint-to-create-sharia-compliant-financial-products-for-the-isdb-member-countries/

www.ingramcontent.com/pod-product-compliance
Lightning Source LLC
LaVergne TN
LVHW041205050326
832903LV00020B/472